Inspirations in
Painted Furniture

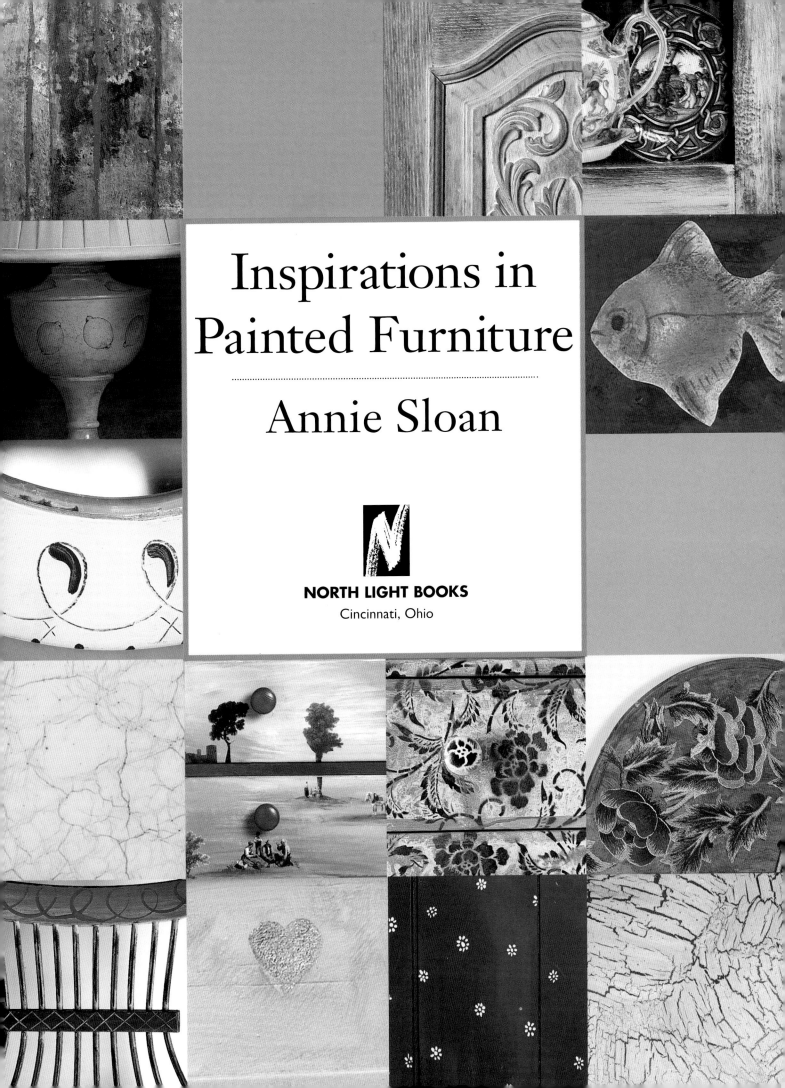

Inspirations in Painted Furniture

Annie Sloan

NORTH LIGHT BOOKS

Cincinnati, Ohio

In memory of Victoria Morland, who knew perfectly how to
paint furniture

Copyright © Collins and Brown Limited 1999
Text copyright © Annie Sloan 1999

First published in North America
in 1999 by North Light Books
an imprint of F&W Publications, Inc.
1507 Dana Avenue
Cincinnati, OH 45207
1-800/289-0963

The right of Annie Sloan to be identified as the author of this work has been
asserted by her in accordance with the Copyright, Designs and Patents Act, 1988.

All rights reserved. No part of this book may be reproduced in any form or by
any electronic or mechanical means including information storage and retrieval
systems without permission in writing from the publisher, except by a reviewer,
who may quote brief passages in a review.

1 3 5 7 9 8 6 2

Library of Congress Cataloging-in-Publication Data;
A catalog record for this book is available.

ISBN 1-58180-006-1

Conceived, edited and designed by Collins and Brown Limited

Editor: Claire Waite
Designers: David Fordham, Claudine Meissner
Photographer: Geoff Dann

Reproduction by Hong Kong Graphic and Printing Ltd, Hong Kong
Printed and bound in China by Sun Fung

Contents

Introduction

HAVE YOU GOT THE PAINTING BUG? Perhaps you are desperate to decorate that unstylish but practical piece of furniture that is found in everybody's house, somewhere. Now is your chance to change it, to make it work within your home and complement the decorative scheme already established there.

The most likely reason for change is that you have a piece of furniture that does not 'gel' with its surroundings, and needs to be integrated into the room. This scenario already provides you with a starting point for choosing colour and, to a certain extent, style. Look through the book to see if you can find something in a similar style; your piece of furniture may be a table, but the technique chosen could be executed on a chair in the book.

Maybe you have been inspired by a friend's efforts, seen something in a magazine or a shop and are now dying to unleash your artistic talents. Perhaps a particular technique has caught your attention and you feel confident to try it. Whatever it is, start with that feeling; your piece of decorated furniture should be a reflection of you.

You may be the type of person who needs a quick result, or perhaps you prefer to take time to savour the experience. Whichever it is, remember that painted furniture does not have to be elaborate, taking an endless amount of time and patience, but taking some trouble and care does pay dividends later. Of course there will be mistakes, and maybe some failures, but don't be put off, persevere and move on to the next piece, returning to repaint the first when you have gained more confidence.

The glory of painting furniture is that literally anything can be painted, from the most unpromising piece of plastic-veneered, mass-produced furniture to a piece specially made for painted furniture enthusiasts. Look out that old unused salad bowl, the unfashionable china vase stuck at the back of the cupboard, the table covered with a cloth because it is stained or the wood is too yellow. Give life to old kitchen cupboards, pinewood furniture and junk-shop finds. Whatever it is, have fun!

Dining room at Charleston

LEFT: Charleston, in Sussex, was home to a group of artists revolving around Duncan Grant and Vanessa Bell. They painted furniture, walls, fabrics and ceramics, culminating in a complete painted house that has been an inspiration to decorative painters ever since. This table, in the dining room, was painted by Vanessa Bell in the 1950s.

Painted Inspirations

PAINTED FURNITURE, whether old or new, has a special place in any room, and these highly individual pieces can reveal tantalizing clues to past owners and events. There is a very rich history of painted furniture, mainly stemming from countries with an abundance of wood and plenty of time to work during long winter evenings. Italy, Eastern Europe and the early settlers of America, for example, have a long tradition of painted furniture, and it is from these that we can look for the inspiration for our own decoration. Traditional painted pieces vary greatly in style, from simple country pieces to rather more classically inspired designs. Use the motifs and colour schemes that appeal to you and integrate them into the materials and techniques you want to use. Do not be afraid to copy a design; the finished result will differ from the original once you have made it your own.

Classical influences

LEFT: In this room the colours are quite neutral and similar in tone. As the rest of the room is unadorned the classically inspired painted designs on the cupboard become the focus of attention. Rosettes, fans and lines are classical motifs found frequently on old painted furniture.

Bold and bright

ABOVE: An unconventional approach to painting chair legs and a table has given this otherwise standard dining furniture a new lease of life. The very bold, simple design works with the bold colours to match a very decorative and stimulating room.

Bloomsbury table

RIGHT: Modern painted furniture begins with a group of artists called the Bloomsbury Group. They worked mainly between the 1930s and 1950s in a bold, free style that has influenced many decorative painters. This table, in the green bathroom at Charleston, their home in Sussex, was decorated by Duncan Grant in the 1930s.

Modern lines

LEFT: The drawers on this very basic chest have been painted with simple lines and blocks of bright colour, giving it a modern look. The decoration was inspired by the other decorative items in the room, such as the vase and candlesticks, and picks up on their colours.

You don't have to look far to the past for inspiration. The artists who lived and worked – from about 1916 to the 1950s – at Charleston, a house in Sussex in the south of England, have influenced many modern decorative painters. Duncan Grant, Vanessa Bell and Roger Fry were among the artists who decorated the interiors, including furniture, in a bold and colourful way, creating designs which have inspired many people to be more adventurous in their decoration. The patterns they used were often abstract or loose interpretations of classical and traditional motifs. For up-to-the-minute inspiration look also at modern art and patterns on contemporary china and fabrics. Modern decoration is usually equated with solely using bright colours, but pale and neutral colours should also be considered: contemporary design tends to use a range of both bright and muted colours. The key to modern decoration is the reliance on shape and line, which tends to be abstract or simplified.

Colour, tone and pattern are the keys to successful decoration. How a piece works against a wall and how it works in a room depends on pattern and tone. There are a few guidelines that can

be considered. The tones on the piece of furniture can be dark, pale, bright or contrasting. A piece painted in contrasting tones will work only in a large room, since the contrasts cause the eye to jump about from dark to light, and so needs a lot of space. A piece decorated in similar tones will tend to merge into the background more easily. This does not mean that the decorations in a small room must be plain. There can be a lot of pattern as long as the colours are not too widely contrasting.

In a busy room, like a kitchen, a piece of furniture painted with elaborate, widely contrasting colours and tones may seem too distracting and unconducive to harmonious life. In this type of situation the decoration should be kept in a tight tonal range or limited to precise areas.

If the walls are very busy and colourful, the furniture needs to be plain, using either patterns in a single tone or just a simple wash of colour. Against plain walls, the furniture may need to be the focus of attention, and can afford to be boldly patterned or colourful. The size of the room also has a bearing on painted furniture. A large room can take an extremely bright, light and busily decorated piece of furniture. Brightly coloured motifs on a dark background, however, are not so dominating and can therefore look good in a small room.

The question of whether your piece of furniture should be decorated in a classical, modern or country style can, to a certain extent, be dictated by the object itself. A simple kitchen chair will never look sophisticated, even if it is gilded and painted with elegant classical designs. It would be much better suited to a contemporary approach or a country-style decoration. A modern, square, 1960s' shelf unit can never look like a bijou 19th-century item. However, there is no reason why such a piece of furniture cannot look stunning, if its decoration takes into consideration the basic qualities of the piece.

When painting furniture to make it look traditional and antiqued, as if it might have come from a great grandparent's attic, there is only one rule: you can reproduce classical designs faithfully only if traditional colours are used. This precludes the use of very bright yellows, sharp greens, purples and electric blues. Colours tended to be more muted and earthy, especially on the cheaper country pieces, while deep reds, warm blues and olive-greens were found on pieces that were more expensive.

Rustic complexity

LEFT: The panels on these kitchen cupboards have been treated with complex hand-painted designs. Each panel, painted by artist Sara Davies, depicts a fat mother hen laying eggs in a straw-filled bower behind hand-painted chicken wire. The effect is comical and charming.

Simple success

ABOVE: Paintwork does not have to be elaborate to work well. Most of the surfaces in this kitchen have been very simply painted with a range of well chosen, soft but strong colours, to give the room great variety. Each chair has been painted a different colour and the panels in the dresser have been picked out in similar shades.

Calming tones

LEFT: Old furniture can appear dark and dominating in modern interiors. To lighten, this wooden chest of drawers white wax has been used. An alternative technique is to brush on paint and wipe it off with a wet sponge before it is dry. The tones of the wall and the chest are kept close in this bedroom, to complete a restful atmosphere.

Delicate decoration

ABOVE: This blue chest has been painted with very fine, delicate classical motifs. To produce work like this takes time and good reference material.

Individual style

RIGHT: This charmingly decorated chest, painted to look like a smart town house, is a clever idea beautifully executed. The colours are muted and subtle so the comical aspect does not become too dominating.

If you have an old house, it does not necessarily mean you have to fill it with traditional designs and aged furniture, and the same is true of a modern home. Contemporary decoration can look excellent when combined with old furniture and classical styles, in fact, mixing styles is one of the easiest processes to get right.

If you are just starting out in decorating, you may feel overwhelmed by the range of terms, techniques and materials. Many of the techniques used to paint furniture today are old favourites reinterpreted in a modern way. Crackle varnish, for instance, is usually seen as a technique that gives painted decoration an authentically old and distressed look, but it can also look distinctly modern, if used over white or cream and worked with aluminium leaf for example. If you are unsure of which technique to use it is best to start where you feel comfortable. Use a technique that inspires you, but one that you also understand, moving to more complex effects as you gain experience.

It is sometimes hard to know when to stop. It is all too easy to go too far and spoil the look you had. Generally, keeping the number of techniques to only two or three prevents the furniture looking too busy. Stop when you can think of nothing more to paint on it or are unsure of the next step. Leave the piece for a while to look at and ponder over. Sometimes leaving it for a day or so and then returning gives you a new perspective on the whole look. Maybe you realize it is perfect as it is or perhaps an extra small line will just finish it off. Varnishing between each layer can be a good idea if possible, that way the last layer can be removed if you are unhappy with it, without damaging the lower layers. This can spoil the spontaneity of your work, which may be an essential part of your enjoyment, but it will prevent later disappointment. Enjoyment is a very important part of decorating furniture so have fun, take your time and the end result will be something you will be proud of for years to come.

Style Directory

Furniture

Accessories

Furniture

INDING FURNITURE TO PAINT is easy, as a glance around almost any home will reveal. Modern pine, melamine, self-assembly pieces, something handed on and pieces from a junk shop are all prime targets for redecoration. Nowadays there is also a lot of furniture made specifically for painting – often from pine or MDF – which requires no preparation and is ready to paint immediately. Old furniture, on the other hand, must be sound before it is painted, so may need some treatment. Always check older pieces, whether from junk shops or inherited from relatives, for woodworm, broken veneers, deep scratches and unstable paintwork or varnish; faults which can all be remedied if spotted before the painting begins.

Workable varnish

This handed-down table was in perfect repair and only needed rubbing down before painting could begin. Coarse sandpaper was used to scratch the table, making an uneven surface or key for the paint to adhere to.

Tough varnish

Like much modern furniture, this headboard has been sprayed with a tough, resin-like varnish, which cannot be removed. Use a matt paint that will adhere easily or apply a commercial priming medium.

Broken structure

This bureau was bought cheaply from a second-hand store because it needed repairing. Simple gluing with white wood glue soon fixed the unstuck leg and broken window frames.

The general shape of the furniture must fit in with the style of decoration: it is difficult to make a stylized 1930s' piece look like a Victorian antique. Either choose an item of furniture based on the decoration you wish to impart, or choose a style of decoration to suit the object in hand. If you already have an item which cannot be jettisoned, and yet does not fit the style criteria, it is a good idea to paint it very plainly so attention is not drawn to it.

Before starting to paint a piece of furniture, take some time to look around for inspiration and ideas. Look in magazines and books, not just at furniture but also at patterns on fabrics and pottery and consider the colours in your room. Once you have decided and work has begun, however, don't be surprised if you are unhappy with the results. This often happens, as ideas don't always work exactly as you imagined. As each stage of the work is completed, stop to reassess it, considering whether the original idea needs adjusting. Don't react too quickly to your decorative paintwork either. Try distancing yourself by positioning the piece in the room it is intended for, or by not looking at it for a short period of time. By then any problems you may have had will be forgotten and you can see the piece with unsullied vision.

Unstuck veneers
The veneer on the top of this old chest was in a very bad state of repair, so it was completely removed. Other broken parts were filled with fine plaster filler until smooth.

Waxed wood
Old and new furniture, particularly old pine, has often been waxed. This wax must be removed before painting can begin, otherwise the new decoration will not adhere and some techniques may be adversely affected.

Chairs

CHAIRS ARE A BASIC ITEM of furniture, yet they are not always the quickest or simplest to decorate. It is easy to unknowingly miss a section and it can be a challenge to decide what will work on awkward areas like legs and struts. Chairs which have reasonable-sized backs or a large seat are perhaps the least perplexing, since they instantly dictate where the focal point of the design should be positioned. If possible, start the decoration on an upside-down chair to ensure you completely cover the legs. When working on the sides and the back you may find it useful to raise the chair on a table.

Glazing and stamping

Painted anywhere and on anything, stripes and checks are guaranteed to cheer up any interior. This traditional chair has been given a modern treatment using a simple striped design. The carvings on the back and legs have deliberately not been picked out, which would be the obvious approach for conventional decoration. Instead, the stripes simply pass straight over them. The choice of colours was influenced by the pink and yellow flecks on the seat fabric.

KEY TO THE TECHNIQUES

Glazing and stamping

Over a **mid-sheen/semi-gloss** light pink base (see p. 62), stripes of dark pink **glaze** (see p. 62) were painted horizontally and vertically. Thinner yellow stripes were **stamped** (see pp. 92–93) using the edge of a piece of cardboard.

Faux marquetry and metal leaf

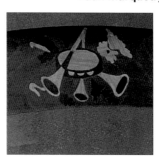

The chair back was adorned with **faux marquetry** (see pp. 116–117), while the turned sections and a curved motif at the edge of the back were gilded with loose Dutch **metal leaf** (see pp. 104–105).

Incising paint

White, brown and grey paints were randomly applied and **incised** (see p. 107) using the end of a paintbrush. White **freehand motifs** (see pp. 97–98) were painted on the seat and back and a **freehand line** (see pp. 100–101) added in grey and white to the back.

Faux marquetry and metal leaf

Although this pretty chair is made from a colourful, warm wood, it was originally unadorned and needed something to bring it to life. Just a little decoration was added, so as not to distract attention from the wood. The design on the back was inspired by traditional marquetry, a method of inlaying woods in simple designs. Two types of wood-effect paper were used, but you could use more. The gilding details were added to balance the decoration.

Incising paint

There are various ways you can choose to give an old item of furniture a lighter, more contemporary look. This chair has been painted with a mixture of light colours and the paintwork broken up with delicate designs that complement the shape of the piece. The loosely executed lattice design on the seat is reminiscent of cane furniture and echoes the decoration on the chair back, giving this piece an attractive refinement.

Freehand decoration

Painted with Russian and medieval decoration, this pew has become a hybrid of the two. The vibrant crimson and scarlet background is reminiscent of luxurious velvet, yet the freehand designs are kept simple and the colours subdued, allowing the red to remain as rich as possible. The small flowers have been painted at random and are bordered by rows of linear decoration above and below. The regular spacing between grass-tuft motifs at the top, which have been positioned centrally above each plank of the pew back, acts as a quiet support to an otherwise quite unconstrained piece.

Freehand painting and incising

These designs were inspired by the decorative style which emerged from Charleston, the home of the Bloomsbury Group, in the 1930s to 1950s. The chairs have been given a bohemian, eccentric style of decoration, using a carefully chosen palette of colours and mixing both simple, abstract motifs and stylized leafy designs. Some of the abstract motifs echo the shapes inherent in the design of the chairs, while some simple doodling adds a lighter touch. In places, texture has been added with the use of layers of paint and visible brushmarks. Both chairs are decorated with terracottas, browns, deep blue, ochre and white, making them similar but not identical.

KEY TO THE TECHNIQUES

Freehand decoration

Deep and bright red **matt** paints (see p. 62) were applied randomly. A light grey glaze was **dragged** (see p. 78) along the top and arm. **Freehand motifs** and **lining** (see pp. 97–98 and 100–101) in off-white, pale blue and grey complete the decoration.

Freehand painting and incising

A blue-green **matt** paint (see p. 62) was **dry brushed** (see p. 73) over white then **freehand motifs** (see pp. 97–98) were added in various colours. In places the still-wet paint was **incised** (see p. 107) using the end of a paintbrush.

Sponging and varnishing

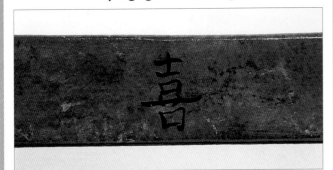

Over a strong pink base, brown and cream glazes were **sponged on** (see p. 75). Chinese letters were **transferred** (see p. 96) to the back and filled in with black paint. Three coats of gloss **varnish** were then applied (see pp. 122–123).

Sponging and varnishing

The design styles of the Orient have long been a source of inspiration to the Western world. The rich colours of the seat fabric and the Chinese characters that adorn it inspired the decoration of this chair. Black-painted Chinese characters stand out proudly against their pink, brown and cream background, while multiple coats of varnish imitate the effect of traditional Chinese lacquerwork. A simple chair is magically reinvented.

Tables

A GOOD PLACE TO display your decorative skills is on a tabletop, since this clear, uninterrupted surface invites all manner of decoration. The style you choose is determined by the type of table you are working with – a simple kitchen table needs a very different treatment to an elegant hall table.

Decoupage and paint effects

Paper cutouts of fish and sea horses dart and dive across a deep blue crackled sea to make a dynamic decoration for this square table. To evoke a natural look of movement some of the fish overlap while others have only a tail or head visible. Turquoise and mid-blue colourwashed waves lap the table legs and sides. A lighter blue frottage over the final arrangement provides a watery veil through which sea creatures can be seen.

KEY TO THE TECHNIQUES

Decoupage and paint effects

On the tabletop, strong blue was **crackleglazed** (see p. 121) over pale blue, and paper fish were **decoupaged** (see pp. 110–111) on top. The legs and sides were **colourwashed** (see p. 76) in turquoise and mid-blue on white. Very dilute paint was then **frottaged** (see p. 80) over the fish.

Gingham and freehand painting

A grid was marked on a white-painted table and alternate squares painted yellow using a flat, wide brush. Illustrations of peas and pea pods were **transferred** (see p. 96) on to the surface. They were then painted **freehand** (see pp. 97–98), following the original illustrations. Writing was added to the side with a calligraphy **pen** and **ink** (see p. 103).

Reverse stencilling

Sign making stickers in a range of sizes were stuck randomly all over the table's **matt** base coats (see p. 62) – blue-green on the base and red-brown on the top – and **reverse stencilled** (see p. 92) in cream patches. The stickers were removed to reveal the base colour as numbers and letters.

Gingham and freehand painting

The pretty, yellow gingham design, adorned with hand-painted little green peas and pods has transformed this very simple square table into a charming, stylish piece, just right for the kitchen. Around the edges, hand-written words in a simple calligraphic style have given the table an extra lift. The thin legs have very little flat surface so long pea pod motifs have been hand-painted on, helping to give a touch of elegance to the table.

Reverse stencilling

Simple numbers and letters, both large and small, take on a playful, almost abstract quality as they lie upside down and on their sides all over this plain table, each figure appearing to burst out of its own spot of colour. The idea for this decoration came from seeing the changing arrangements of childrens' magnetic letters on the refrigerator door. The decoration was executed, however, using sticky plastic letters for sign making, bought from a stationer's.

Dragging and freehand lining

The design of this table suggested a classical Italian style of decoration, and since its shape is strong, the decoration was kept simple. To define its elegant slenderness the table was dragged using a pale glaze over a vibrant base. Simple painted lines along all the edges are designed to delineate the classical shape and emphasize the curves of the cabriole legs. The straight back legs suggest that this table could be positioned with its back to the wall, and would look wonderful in a hallway or at the edge of any room.

Ivory crackle varnish

Ivory is the theme of this unusual table and echoes the elephants which act as its supports. The top, treated with a cracking varnish, is reminiscent of old yellowed and crazed ivory and gives an elegance and lightness to an otherwise heavy piece of furniture. The pale colour also contributes, making the table appear less bulky than its former natural wood incarnation. The base has been discreetly aged with elephant grey paint, for a more solid look.

Metal leaf and stamping

This well-worn kitchen table was pitted, marked and retained remnants of previous paintwork – even after applying a number of coats of paint stripper – so it needed to be decorated in a style that would complement these aged characteristics. To emphasize the unusual matt patina and delicate, soft colour of the tabletop, contrasting strips of shiny aluminium and copper leaf were wrapped around the table edge. The leaf was deliberately torn to give a worn, jagged finish while printed lines across the width of the table pull the loose shapes together.

KEY TO THE TECHNIQUES

Dragging and freehand lining

Over a terracotta-red base, greyed-green glaze was **dragged** (see p. 78). A light green **freehand line** (see pp. 100–101) was painted along every edge and a thin line in dark green and then red was added to pick out the curve of each cabriole leg.

Ivory crackle varnish

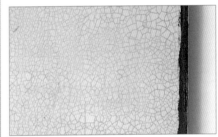

An off-white base was crazed with **crackle varnish** (see p. 120). The base was **varnished** and **distressed** (see p. 119) with steel wool and grey paint. The edges of the tabletop were roughly painted with diluted grey paint.

Metal leaf and stamping

Torn strips of aluminium and copper **metal leaf** (see pp. 104–105) were applied at the edge of the table and **distressed** (see p. 106). Rough blue stripes were **stamped** with cardboard (see pp. 92–93).

Chests

CHESTS OF DRAWERS come in all shapes and sizes and there are many ways to decorate them. Drawers can be treated differently to the rest of the chest or each drawer treated differently from the next, or the whole chest can be covered with a single decoration, without drawing attention to drawers or doors.

Glossy glaze paints

Three panels of vivid red and orange surrounded by a sea of stormy blue transform a plain chest into a bold, modern statement. Inspired by the American painter Mark Rothko, whose large, abstract canvases depict similar colours and shapes, the effect is achieved using a glossy but partly transparent paint in strong vibrant colours. Many layers of overlapping paint create great depth and, in places, produce a subtle blend of colours.

KEY TO THE TECHNIQUES

Glossy glaze paints

Red, orange, blue and green **glossy glaze paints** (see p. 72) were applied in alternate layers and overlapped in places.

Potato stamping and distressing

Designs cut from a potato were **stamped** (see p. 95) in terracotta over yellow ochre. Blue paint was **distressed with wax** (see p. 118) around the edges.

Painted sky

Over a white base, a **sky** effect (see p. 82) was applied. For ease of work and continuity the drawer handles were removed and the drawers opened a little.

Potato stamping and distressing

The textural qualities of the paintwork on this chest are what makes the simple design and colouring so special. The printed patterns, made by combining basic diamond and rectangle motifs, are deliberately irregular and were inspired by African decoration. A potato was used as the stamping tool, since the starch in the vegetable gives it the unique quality of variously accepting and resisting paint, making an individual and uneven print every time.

Painted sky

A softly painted sky with delicate summery clouds transforms this simple chest of drawers. Its hard, angular shape is softened by wispy stippled clouds, which will look equally effective in a modern setting – something reminiscent of Magritte's surreal paintings – or a pretty, dreamy bedroom. You can also adapt the design by adding other colours to suggest different moods and times of day, such as pinkish tones for evening light or dark tones for a night sky.

Spray stencilling and frottage

A Japanese-inspired pattern of delicate flowers is softened by a veil of blue, as if a piece of lacy chiffon has been thrown over this small chest of drawers. Spray paints were chosen for this stencil design because of the light, fine, textured finish they impart. The dramatic look of a black design over a white base is softened by a blue frottage, creating patches of darker and lighter colour, which sometimes almost obliterate the design underneath.

Stone effect and decoupage

In keeping with the formal nature of a bureau, this piece has been decorated with a finish that looks solid and sober, yet contemporary. The colours are cool and the techniques simple. The sponged, stone-look paintwork in several tones of grey, beige and white matches the classical paper frieze on the drawer fronts, toned down and aged with a little diluted paint. Multiple coats of matt varnish disguise the edge of the cut-out frieze.

KEY TO THE TECHNIQUES

Spray stencilling and frottage

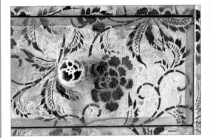

The chest was painted with white **mid-sheen/semi-gloss** paint (see p. 62) and **spray stencilled** (see p. 91) in black. A mid-blue **frottage** (see p. 80) was then applied all over. A single flower was spray stencilled in black on the drawer handles.

Stone effect and decoupage

Over a beige base, three tones of greyed-beige glaze were **sponged on** (see p. 75). A paper frieze was lightly coloured with a little diluted grey-brown paint and **decoupaged** (see pp. 110–111) to the drawer fronts.

Roller stencilling

A grid design was **roller stencilled** (see p. 91) in blue and lilac over a beige **matt** base (see p. 62). Using a roller again, flower stencils were randomly printed in blues, greens, browns, reds, ochres and purples, overprinting in some areas.

Roller stencilling

A contemporary look has been produced on a plain chest of drawers by combining abstract, linear motifs with stylized flowers and leaves. The overall design has actually been applied quite randomly, using three stencils, a roller and several colours. Although predominantly based around blue, other colours such as emerald, crimson, scarlet, brown and ochre have also been used to lift the effect. The flower stencils have been applied over the first grid stencil, sometimes overprinting leaves and flowers but always leaving a little space for the design to 'breathe'. The result is an almost abstract effect.

Cabinets and Cupboards

CABINETS AND CUPBOARDS are essential items of furniture, but they are often large and dominating. You can tackle their decoration in two ways. Either merge them in with the rest of the room by decorating with a single colour or with one technique, or turn them into the focus of attention by decorating with several different techniques and a range of colours.

KEY TO THE TECHNIQUES

Colourwash and metal leaf

The white-painted cabinet was **colourwashed** (see p. 76) with a grey-brown glaze. Gold size was painted on in heart and diamond shapes and gilded using loose Dutch **metal leaf** (see pp. 104–105). The cabinet was finished with a coat of matt **varnish** (see pp. 122–123).

Tartan and decoupage

Over a purple base, mid-green glaze was applied in a **tartan** design (see p. 81). Red and green **freehand lines** (see pp. 100–101) finish the effect. The central panel was **decoupaged** (see pp. 110–111) using manuscript wrapping paper.

Stencilling and freehand painting

Pink and terracotta **matt** paints (see p. 62) were applied with a **dry brush** (see p. 73). A row of **three-dimensional effect** (see p. 98) pink balls was painted freehand along the base. Stencils were **stippled with a brush** (see p. 90) in greyed-white and shadows and highlights were hand-painted in.

Colourwash and metal leaf

White and gold pair together beautifully and this classic combination has transformed this simple bathroom cabinet. For a natural look, varied brush strokes have been used and remain visible in the decoration. The imperfections of the wood can also still be seen. Very light, subtle colourwashing gives the cabinet a weathered look, and the gold motifs, symbolic of love and money, have a rough quality which complements the texture of the surrounding paint.

Colourwash and metal leaf

Tartan and decoupage

By reproducing a tartan pattern you can introduce a variety of colours to an interior, whether they be cool and restrained or loud and vibrant. By varying the width and position of the stripes and overlapping glazes to produce many different colours, you can make your tartans, plaids and checks almost infinite in their possibilities. Here, the Latin manuscript decoupaged in the recess has a stripy pattern that provides the perfect foil to the tartan.

Stencilling and freehand painting

This country-style corner shelf has been painted to resemble some of the folk art furniture from Northern Europe. Along the base runs a small row of hand-painted balls, like a necklace of pearls, and down the sides and along the top leaf-shaped arabesques echo and complement the shelf design. The pink and terracotta dry-brushed base coat provides the perfect textured background to the solid colour of the stencils and freehand motifs.

Liming

The pale, misty, grey-brown decoration of this carved oak sideboard belies its heaviness. Many large pieces of furniture started life coated in a thick, orange-brown varnish that made them appear dark and weighty. Once this treacly coat is removed the feel of the furniture beneath can easily be reversed. In this case the oak has been made to look light, cool and surprisingly delicate by the application of white wax, made stronger in the carved panels. This treatment works particularly well on oak because the coloured wax emphasizes its distinctively deep, pronounced and varied grain.

Distressing and waxing

A new kitchen can look clinical and cold. To add texture and warmth you can give your cabinets an aged effect. In order to conjure up the nostalgic look of an old Victorian dairy, the colour of buttermilk, cheese and clotted cream was chosen for these kitchen cupboards. In the places which usually see a lot of use, the original wood is revealed, while the application of a little dark wax adds extra texture and colour. The beauty of this finish is that the natural wear and tear sustained in a kitchen only serves to make the effect more authentic.

Dragging

Built-in cupboards can present quite a problem when it comes to decoration, since they usually have little architectural shape or interest. The cupboards in this bedroom have been painted to blend with the wall, using a lighter tone of the wall colour, but made more interesting by emphasizing the panels. The mix of colour – a yellowed-green – and technique – dragging – is classically English in style, and is emphasized by the sharp white mouldings and door handles. Alternatively, use greyed-blue, deep golden ochre or greyed-brown to achieve the same traditional look.

KEY TO THE TECHNIQUES

Liming

After **removing the varnish** (see p. 68) the sideboard was **limed** (see p. 125). More white wax was used in the central carved areas than on the rest of the piece. Several times a year this is revitalized with a coat of beeswax.

Distressing and waxing

Buttermilk paint was **distressed with wax** (see p. 118) around the handles and areas that usually get knocked. A little dark **wax** (see p. 124) has been worked into the corners and mouldings.

Dragging

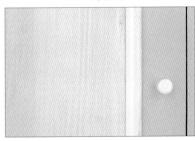

Over a white base, a green glaze was lightly **dragged** (see p. 78) on the door surrounds. On the panels the same glaze was dragged more strongly, removing more glaze and producing a lighter, more transparent colour.

Stamping and penwork

Like chessboards and traditional floor tiles, black chequered patterns always look smart, and they work particularly well against the neutral brown of wood. This cupboard was completed in two stages, and although the designs match, the techniques are quite different. The base decoration took time and patience to complete, using pen and ink to produce a clean, sharp look. On the top a sponge was used to imitate the base decoration, with much softer results.

Trompe l'oeil decoupage

Glancing at this cupboard, it seems that the shelves behind the glass door are laden with beautiful china plates and jugs. Closer inspection reveals, however, that these are paper cutouts from art magazines, stuck down on to paper 'shelves'. The cutouts overlap and some can only partly be seen, as if the shelves are jam-packed with ornaments. The effect is like a trompe l'oeil painting that deceives the eye, but is much easier to execute.

Print room technique and combing

Print rooms needn't be confined to walls. This very plain cupboard has been transformed into something quite exotic and grand by the addition of black and white prints framed with decorative borders, along with painted lines and coloured backgrounds. Armed with a pile of prints from an old encyclopedia, the theme of foreign lands was born, and the formal elements of a traditional print room were deliberately combined with the informal style of freehand painting.

KEY TO THE TECHNIQUES

Stamping and penwork

Black, orange and light brown squares were **stamped with a sponge** (see p. 94) to form a checked pattern on the top of the cupboard.

A design was **transferred** (see p. 96) to the central panel of the base and a checked pattern marked around it in pencil. The **basic penwork** technique was used to fill in the checks and the design completed by **filling in the background** with ink (see pp. 102–103)

Trompe l'oeil decoupage

Pictures of crockery – roughly in proportion to each other – were **decoupaged** (see pp. 110–111) on to the rich brown cupboard door. The rest of the cupboard was **dry brushed** (see p. 73) with **matt** pale blue-grey paint (see p. 62).

Print room technique and combing

At the top, red and blue glazes were **combed** (see p. 79) over yellow and a repeating flower motif **roller stencilled** (see p. 91) in blue. The **print room technique** (see pp. 112–113) was used on the doors and **freehand lines** (see pp. 100–101) of several widths and colours added around the edges.

Distressing with wax

The rich blue on this substantial dresser makes it colourful and friendly, transforming a standard piece of pine furniture into something unique. This particular shade of blue emphasizes the warmth of the pine which is revealed in the areas where the paint has been distressed. A strong colour like this also makes a wonderful backdrop for displaying colourful china. Warm blue-greens, grey-blues and pale sage greens also work well with old pine.

Symmetrical decoupage

This vibrant dresser has all the brightness and boldness of Eastern European folk art. The bold gypsy colours of pink, deep red and orange, with blue dots and symmetrical vases of flowers cut from abstract patterned wrapping paper, combine to make a piece that is lively and perhaps a little loud. These strong colours are best positioned against a bold background and such decoration should be complemented with distinctive crockery and ornaments.

KEY TO THE TECHNIQUES

Distressing with wax

The pine dresser was coated with a rich blue paint and **distressed with wax** (see p. 118) around the areas that usually get the most use.

Symmetrical decoupage

Pink and deep red **matt** paints (see p. 62) were **dry brushed** on (see p. 73) and **symmetrical designs** (see p. 115) decoupaged in the panels. Roughly applied **freehand lines** and **motifs** (see pp. 100–101 and 97–98) in red, orange and blue adorn the panels and drawers, with patches of orange added around the edges.

Headboards

BED HEADBOARDS ARE perfect for decoration, whether on a double or single bed, since they consist of a large flat space often contained within a 'frame'. Headboards vary in shape and size much less than most pieces of furniture, although one may have posts like a traditional American bed, or you may even work with a four poster. Whatever style of headboard you choose to decorate, remember that the pillows may cover some of the design, so make sure the main part of the decoration is high enough to be seen. The bedcover pattern should also be considered.

As well as the headboard, many beds also have a footboard, which may be seen on both sides depending how the bed is placed in the room. It is a good idea to repeat the decoration from the headboard on the footboard, perhaps on a smaller scale.

KEY TO THE TECHNIQUES

Patchwork decoupage

White then bright blue **mid-sheen/semi-gloss** paints (see p. 62) were applied and squares of wrapping paper **decoupaged** (see pp. 110–111) in a chequered arrangement. The blue paint was rubbed away in places with a damp sponge.

Pearlized stencilling

Over a deep blue **matt** base (see p. 62) green-blue was **frottaged** (see p. 80). The border was stencilled by **stippling with a brush** (see p. 90), using green **pearlized paint** (see p. 73). A little pearlized paint was applied to the posts.

Gilding and incising

Dutch **metal leaf** (see pp. 104–105) was applied to the panels and top and parts were **distressed** (see p. 106). The top was **incised** (see p. 107) through blue and brown paint. **Matt** blue (see p. 62) was painted around the panels.

Patchwork decoupage

Inspired by a traditional craft steeped in history and nostalgia, this headboard has been decorated with a patchwork design. Instead of using old scraps of fabric, however, squares of floral papers have been collected. This design uses a simple chequered effect with five different papers, but, armed with books of patchwork designs, a wide range of different patterns and colour arrangements can be tried. Many traditional designs such as 'log cabin', 'star' and 'Roman square' can be effectively adapted to decoupage.

Pearlized stencilling

An old-fashioned American headboard has been treated to a snappy, modern look. By day, the matt-textured overall finish contrasts with the silvery, pearlized stencilling and details, and the piece looks clean and cool. At night, the stencil decoration becomes more reflective and the focus of attention, giving the headboard a glamourous, chic look. The stencil design, an abstract motif with Celtic overtones, makes a simple arch that follows the shape of the headboard.

Gilding and incising

A splendid, antique-looking headboard was made from old pieces of wood salvaged from a reclamation yard. The combination of the colours used to decorate it and the classical European woodwork results in a unique piece of furniture. The colours, blue, brown and gold, are reminiscent of Eastern fabrics and temples and give the piece a richness that matches its exotic design. The coolness of blue and the warmth of the brown perfectly complement the gold. To aid the general antique look the old, flaking paint has been retained in places, but repainted and gilded in others.

Accessories

T HE SMALL PIECES in a room – boxes, lampbases and shades, frames, trays, candlesticks and bowls – accentuate the style and colour of their surroundings. These small items are also most susceptible to changes in fashion, so you may want to revitalize them frequently, a necessity which provides a great opportunity, or perhaps an excuse, to paint the accessories in

the home. Small items are also great to decorate and give as presents. An individual, hand-decorated box or bowl has a personal touch that is always appreciated and treasured.

You will find furniture accessories suitable for painting in all manner of places. Raid the kitchen cupboards for glass bowls and plates, and look out old vases. Old cigar boxes, tin trays and plastic

New varnished wood

This new wooden salad bowl had a varnish on it that has been removed. Paint will now adhere well to it, and the danger of the decoration chipping off if the object gets a lot of use is reduced.

Plastic

If a plastic object is too shiny to paint, try scratching it with coarse steel wool to make a good key. Although very light-weight, plastic objects have great decorative potential and can be cleverly disguised.

New wood

Pine is a common new wood and since it is cheap and plentiful it is often painted. New pine has little grain and absorbs paints and varnishes easily. This may make it necessary to seal the surface before decorating.

Painted wood

New and old wooden objects are often painted. If the paint is chipping away it will need to be stripped, but stable paintwork only requires sanding to make a good key.

Old varnished wood

This old lampbase, like many old pieces, is coated with a varnish and simply needs rubbing down with coarse steel wool or sandpaper, making a good key for the new paint to adhere to.

frames can be turned into something unique. Many items, known as 'blanks', are sold solely to be decorated, and need no preparation before painting. Junk shops are bound to provide a range of items that can be transformed with a judicious lick of paint, while a lot of new items can be bought from cut-price shops, especially when decorating on a tight budget. Plastic frames, often moulded into very grand designs, are usually sprayed with an unpleasant gold colour, but they can easily be painted or gilded with metal leaf and used to make an excellent decorative focus for a room. Boxes can be bought made from a fine cardboard which is very easy to decorate. Any material can be painted, including plastic, although check that it is not too shiny before you buy since in that state the water-based paint will have difficulty adhering successfully.

The accessories are fun, easy, cheap and quick to decorate. Because they are small they can be worked with on the kitchen table without too much fuss, and since they are inexpensive you will find yourself under less pressure to get the decoration right first time. Even if your first attempt is unsuccessful, it will not take long to repaint it with something new, so why not try out some new techniques on the accessories in your home?

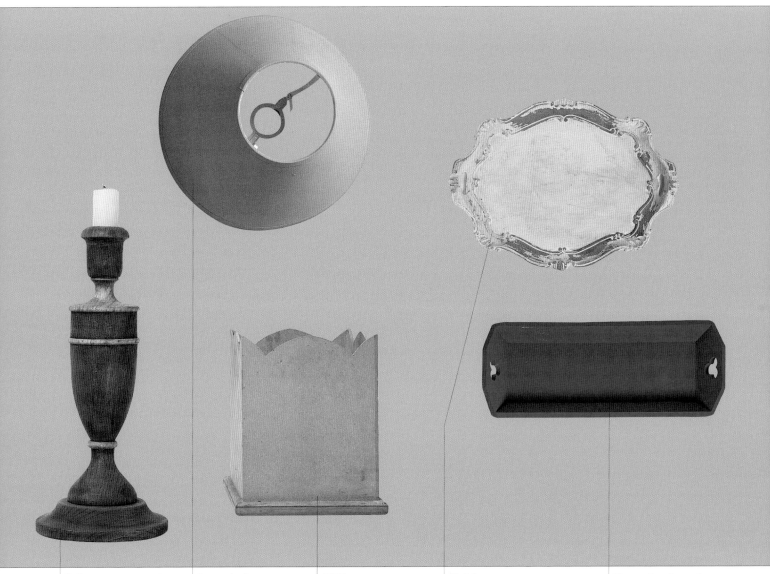

Oak

Oak is a very hard wood with a deep grain which may need to be filled if you do not want it to continually show through the new decoration. This is particularly important for fine techniques like using crackle varnish.

Lampshades

Lampshades are made from either fabric or parchment. Fabric is usually very absorbent so it may need to be sealed before painting. This will make it opaque so when the bulb is on the light does not shine through the shade.

MDF

MDF is a modern, strong product with a smooth surface, sometimes considered to be lacking in character. However, it makes a great surface for painting. MDF should be cut professionally.

Metal

Tin objects such as trays and jugs are easily found in junk shops. They may need to be treated for rust before decorating. Some metals, like galvanized zinc, do not rust and are ideal for painting.

New painted wood

A newly painted, matt wooden object needs no preparation. If, on the other hand, the paint is glossy, the surface should be sanded to remove the shine, ensuring the new decoration will adhere.

Boxes

THE SURFACES OF A BOX almost demand to be painted, with the lid asking for special attention. The chosen decoration can be in imitation of luxurious materials such as tortoiseshell, marble or expensive woods, or you can create simple, informal or classic effects using decoupage, stencilling or freehand painting. These styles of decoration can be extended to other objects which have similar uses, such as an open pencil box or filing tray, string boxes, wastepaper baskets and umbrella stands.

Dragging
The mock panels of this plain wastepaper basket emphasize its tapered shape. This traditional English colour combination uses three tones of olive-green, with the palest in the centre.

Coloured tortoiseshell
Real tortoiseshell was sometimes stained red or green, so, to give this wastepaper basket a touch of elegance, a pale and dark green tortoiseshell has been applied.

Painted tortoiseshell
Real and painted tortoiseshell has been used on boxes and frames for hundreds of years. In the panel of this box, the reddish-brown shell markings radiate from one corner. Elsewhere, the diagonal marks are smaller and more contained.

Geometric decoupage
Little geometric shapes cover the surface of this box giving it a contemporary look. The intricate-looking pattern is simply made by cutting triangles, squares and arches from folded paper.

Faux marquetry
A popular method of displaying woods with different colours and grains is to insert shapes cut from wooden veneers into the wood. The real thing can often be seen on small boxes like this, but here the effect is imitated using paper.

Combing
A striking arrangement of black stripes and wavy lines over a multicoloured base results in a contemporary and chic effect. The base colours shine through the combed glaze and both soften and enliven the black.

Dragging and metallic paint
This open-topped box has been dragged with a reddish-brown glaze to look like mahogany. The gold words, written in an old-fashioned script, keep the whole piece understated and discreet.

Bird's-eye maple

Inexpensive, plain boxes can be disguised as ornate objects made from precious and interesting woods. This little box has been transformed by painted woodgraining, imitating bird's-eye maple.

Decoupage

A mass of flowers covers the lid of this hexagonal box, and on the sides animals hide in the giant flowers, fruit and foliage. When the box is closed the pictures join up.

Painted marble

A marbled effect on a box gives it a feeling of weight and solidity. This wooden treasure chest already had a romantic, theatrical look which has been heightened and emphasized by a dramatic marble effect.

KEY TO THE TECHNIQUES

Painted tortoiseshell

Although treated separately, the panel and edges were both painted with a **tortoiseshell** effect (see p. 85).

Geometric decoupage

Geometric designs (see p. 115) were glued to a white box then **matt** grey-blue paint (see p. 62) was rubbed back with a damp sponge.

Faux marquetry

This lid was decorated with **faux marquetry** (see pp. 116–117) using three papers.

Combing

Over a multicoloured **variegated** base (see p. 73), black glaze was **combed** (see p. 79).

Dragging and metallic paint

Red-brown glaze was **dragged** (see p. 78) and gold **metallic paint** (see p. 109) added.

Dragging

Dark and olive-green glazes were **dragged** (see p. 78) over pale green.

Coloured tortoiseshell

A **tortoiseshell** effect (see p. 85) was applied using shades of dark green.

Decoupage

Motifs were **decoupaged** (see pp. 110–111) so that they met between lid and base.

Bird's-eye maple

Over cream, light tan glaze was grained to imitate **bird's-eye maple** (see p. 83).

Painted marble

A **marble** effect (see pp. 84–85) was applied using white and ochre over black.

Curtain Poles

KEY TO THE TECHNIQUES

Metallic wax
A commercially bought pewter **metallic wax** was applied (see p. 109) over a **matt** black base (see p. 62). and buffed with a soft cloth.

Distressed gilding
Over dark grey, aluminium **metal leaf** was lightly **distressed** (see p. 106). Green **freehand lines** were added (see pp. 100–101) and green paint on the finial wiped off with a cloth.

Decoupage
Tissue paper motifs were **decoupaged** (see pp. 110–111) around the white pole and areas embellished with **freehand motifs** (see pp. 97–98).

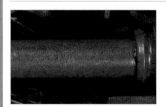

Stippling
Over a strong, mid-green base coat, black glaze was **stippled** (see p. 77).

Gilding and freehand painting
Over a terracotta base, Dutch **metal leaf** was lightly **distressed** (see p. 106). A motif was **transferred** to the pole (see p. 96) and filled in with paint.

Dragging
Blue glaze was **dragged** (see p. 78) over a silver **metallic** paint base (see p. 109).

Metal leaf
Dutch **metal leaf** (see pp. 104–105) was applied to the raised areas of the finial. The whole pole was **varnished** with a gloss varnish (see pp. 122–123).

URTAIN POLES can be decorated like any other accessory, and provided it is well varnished, the decoration will be protected from damage from the rings. A good place to start when considering the decoration is with the curtain fabric. You can either choose colours that match the fabric and so blend in, or colours which contrast so that the pole stands out.

Metallic wax
Pewter, like bronze, is a dark-coloured metal suited, generally, to robustly designed objects. In keeping with the solid baronial look of this finial a pewter look was chosen.

Distressed gilding
This ornate curtain pole, with its lavish sea serpent finial, has been given a contemporary twist by using green and silver over a dark grey. A more traditional way to treat this subject would be to use reds and gold.

Decoupage

A winding vine of fruit or flowers is a classic way to decorate a pole, whether it's a curtain pole, bedpost or even a lampbase. Hand-painting is the traditional method but using decoupage techniques makes an effective and interesting alternative.

Metal leaf

When wood and gold are used together the one perfectly complements the other because they work together rather than competing for attention. Three parts of this finial have been picked out to show the wood to its greatest advantage.

Stippling

This curtain pole has been given strength and depth with the addition of a stippled effect. A strong, bright base coat is the secret ingredient of bold paint effects.

Gilding and freehand painting

The grapevine that winds around this gilded curtain pole has been carefully hand-painted and looks exquisite. If you are not confident with your freehand painting ability you could try using acetate stencils for a similar effect.

Dragging

Each facet of the bought mosaic finial is picked out in a different colour, like a harlequin's jacket. The decoration uses one of those colours, the blue, dragged loosely along its length and adding colour without being too overpowering against the finial.

Lampbases and Lampshades

WELL-DECORATED LAMPSHADE or lampbase helps to set the style of a room, since it is often these details that the eye unknowingly focuses on. There are many plain and undistinguished bases and shades on the market, or already in our homes, and these could be dramatically or subtly transformed by decoration; the plain could become ornate, the simple could become grand and the ordinary become quite unique. This means that a well-shaped base or shade in the wrong colour or pattern can be cleverly redecorated to suit the rest of your room.

Stone effect

The classical column has been a traditional lampbase shape for many years. A popular form of decoration for this design is a stone effect that makes the piece appear appropriately heavy, like a miniature stone column.

Spray stencilling

A plain lampshade can be decorated to match the fabrics or stencilling in a room, obliterating little light. Here, an interesting silhouette can be seen on the shade when the lamp is in use.

Combing

A simple wooden lampbase has been painted with a stronger, darker and more obvious woodgrained effect, to give it weight and solidity. The different-sized stripes, made with a graduated comb, look like the natural grain of wood.

Freehand painting and crackle varnish

The wide surfaces on this bulbous-shaped lampbase allow great scope for decoration. Here, delicately hand-painted lemons adorn the base, while crackle varnish tones down the yellow and suggests a look of old china.

Painted marble

Marbling is an unusual effect for a lampshade, and looks great in a room needing low, atmospheric light. For a realistic, solid stone look, the lampshade was painted with many base coats, to make sure no light shines through.

Tartan

When this lamp is on, the light shines through the semi-transparent glaze on the shade so that the colours glow, and, where there is no glaze, there are small areas of extra brightness.

Metallic paint and decoupage

Copper and malachite-green were popular colours in the 1930s, inspired by the popularity of Egyptian art at the time. On this little lampbase, the 1930s' flavour is also emphasized by the simple diamond shapes cut from paper.

KEY TO THE TECHNIQUES

Stone effect
Over a cream-painted base coat, ochre, light brown and off-white glazes were **sponged on** (see p. 75).

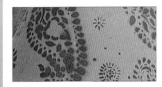

Spray stencilling
Dark green was **spray stencilled** (see p. 91) through a fine stencil design on to a light green lampshade.

Combing
An opaque brown glaze was **combed** (see p. 79) down the column and across the base of this wooden lampbase, using a graduated comb.

Freehand painting and crackle varnish
Over a cream base, lemon motifs were **transferred** (see p. 96) and painted **freehand** (see pp. 96–98). The lampbase was then **crackle varnished** (see p. 120).

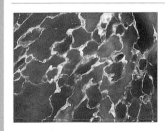

Painted marble
Several coats of dark green, **mid-sheen/semi-gloss** paint (see p. 62) were applied. The shade was **marbled** (see p. 84) using dark and mid-green glazes, and white paint for the veins.

Metallic paint and decoupage
Over a coat of copper **metallic paint** (see p. 109) simple shapes cut from malachite-effect paper were **decoupaged** (see pp. 110–111).

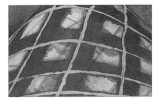

Tartan
The white lampshade was given a **tartan** effect (see p. 81) using green glaze. **Freehand lines** (see pp. 100–101) in yellow and red were added.

Frames

FRAMES ARE OFTEN sold commercially already adorned with painted motifs or other decorative features, but plain, unadorned picture and mirror frames can be easily elaborated with your own decoration, and their usually flat surfaces allow for all kinds of experimentation. Generally, the larger and more demanding the picture in terms of colour and activity, the quieter the frame decoration should be. A mirror frame, on the other hand, can afford to be elaborate, colourful and generally busier than a frame for a picture.

Distressed gilding

The flashes of blue seen through the gold on this elegant moulded frame, give this traditional distressed effect a contemporary feel. Emerald-green, purples and reds are also excellent as contemporary bases for metallic finishes.

Dragging

Like an open-weave, silky fabric, this pretty blue and white frame looks soft and delicate. A light frame like this would suit a dark, bold picture.

Stamping

Inspired by Maori tattoos, the enormous spirals curl around and overlap the frame, making it a piece that really catches the eye.

Stripes

Candy stripes in pink or other pastel colours – like blue-green and lilac – have a young and fresh look about them: the colours are very clear and the design is simple. You can either mix wide and thin widths of stripes, or keep to regular widths, as here.

Metal leaf and stamping

The distressed gilding on this plain frame is inspired by old frames whose gold decoration has worn away in places, revealing a terracotta-red base. The blue lines break up the flatness of the frame creating tension and energy.

Frottage and decoupage
Black and white 19th-
century prints of insects
and small animals crawl
around this dark frame.
The two colours used as a
background and to lightly
tint the cutouts add warmth
and give the cutouts an
extra dimension.

Repeat stencilling
A range of colours in
different-shaped patches
produces an abstract effect
on this plain frame. The
strong colours make a rich
frame for the black and
white print. Paler colours
could be used to frame a
stronger coloured picture.

Combing pearlized paint
Pearly green iridescent
wavy stripes radiate light
from the frame and give
focus to the print it
surrounds. As the light
catches the green pearlized
paint it picks up on the red
of the frame, producing a
pinkish blush.

KEY TO THE TECHNIQUES

Dragging
Over a pale blue base, white
glaze was **dragged** (see p. 78)
in one direction then, when dry, in
a second direction.

Stamping
On to a green **matt** base (see
p. 62) light blue was **stamped**
using two symmetrical stamps
cut from polystyrene (see p. 95).

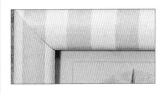

Stripes
On a white **mid-sheen/semi-
gloss** base coat (see p. 62), pink
stripes were painted using
masking tape (see p. 100).

Distressed gilding
Over a bright blue **matt** base
coat (see p. 62), Dutch **metal
leaf** was lightly **distressed**
(see p. 106).

Frottage and decoupage
Deep blue was **frottaged** (see
p. 80) over deep pink and lightly
coloured (see p. 113) black and
white cutouts **decoupaged** (see
pp. 110–111) around the frame.

Metal leaf and stamping
Over a **matt** terracotta base (see
p. 62), Dutch **metal leaf** was
distressed (see p. 106). Blue
lines were **stamped** using
cardboard (see pp. 92–93).

Repeat stencilling
The motif was **stencilled with a
roller** (see p. 91) in random
positions and using many
colours, over a dark red base.

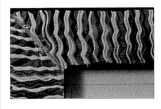

Combing pearlized paint
Over a green base, red glaze
was **combed** (see p. 79).
When dry, green **pearlized
paint** (see p. 73) was combed
over the top.

Stencilling and bronze powders

A cascade of shimmering leaves falls down the sides of this mirror. The leaves are coloured with bronze powders that glint in the light giving a dramatic look. The stencilled leaves are the same colour as the background so, in certain lights, they almost disappear, becoming a shadowy matt image. Used on contrasting colours the matt colour would be more apparent. Yet, as you walk past the mirror, the light catches the leaves making them bright and shiny. These metallic powders on furniture are wonderful for rooms used only at night, for a hint of glamour.

Incising and freehand painting

Like doodles, childrens' drawings and writing exercises, a freely drawn looped line moves expressively around this mirror frame, accentuating its inherent shape and producing a vivacious, lively and modern item of furniture. The incising technique used here is worked with wet paint, so if you make a mistake it can be easily painted out and begun again. This also means you are safe to lose your inhibitions and let yourself work in an unconstrained style. The thin, gold inner band gives the whole piece a chic touch.

KEY TO THE TECHNIQUES

Stencilling and bronze powders

The frame was **dry brushed** (see p. 73) in terracotta-brown and slate-blue. A **stencil** (see p. 88) was drawn through in pencil and red-copper and yellow-gold **bronze powders** (see p. 108) applied to the design.

Incising and freehand painting

Over a dark red base, white **matt** paint (see p. 62) was applied and, while still wet, **incised** (see p. 107) with loops and crosses using the end of a paintbrush. Blue **freehand motifs** (see pp. 97–98) were added and Dutch **metal leaf** (see pp. 104–105) was applied in a line around the inside edge of the frame.

Woodgraining and decoupage

Over a pale yellow base, mid-brown glaze was applied to imitate the **bird's-eye maple woodgrain** (see p. 83). Flowers cut from wrapping paper were **decoupaged** (see pp. 110–111) all around the frame, sometimes overlapping each other and bending around the moulding at the edge.

Woodgraining and decoupage

In Victorian England flowers and leaves in the form of garlands and borders were popular motifs, usually painted over pretty wooden furniture. Here, the idea has been revived, but with a twist. Instead of freehand painting, paper cutouts have been used, while the wooden background is also a little deceptive; the mirror originally had a plain pine frame, which has been greatly enhanced by adding a woodgrain effect, suggesting a richer and more interesting wood.

Trays

KEY TO THE TECHNIQUES

Colourwashing and stamping
Mauve was **colourwashed** (see p. 76) over lilac in places and a brown **masking tape line** (see p. 100) added. Orange, brown and blue dots were **stamped** with a cork (see pp. 92–93).

Decoupage and hand-painting
Fishy cutouts were **decoupaged** (see pp. 110–111) and **freehand motifs** (see pp. 97–98) painted in blue and off-white to give the illusion of water.

Lining with pearlized paint
Over a dark blue base, **masking tape lines** (see p. 100) and **freehand motifs** (see pp. 97–98) were painted in blue **pearlized paint** (see p. 73).

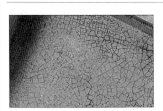

Crackle varnish
Crackle varnish (see p. 120) was applied over a **matt** yellow-brown base (see p. 62).

Masking fluid
Over a black base, the outline of a face and edging lines were painted in **masking fluid** (see p. 99). The details were added and the masking fluid lifted off.

Sponging and metal leaf
Over a terracotta base, mauve, green and blue were **sponged on** (see p. 75) to depict a scene. Dutch **metal leaf** was **distressed** (see p. 106) around the rim.

Roller stencilling
A checked design was painted on in reddish-brown and green **matt** diluted paint (see p. 62). A leaf design was randomly **roller stencilled** (see p. 91) all over the tray.

IT IS POSSIBLE TO DECORATE a tray using almost any technique, although a finish which involves using wax is not totally practical; any water spilt on the waxed decoration will mark the effect. Whichever finish you choose it is a good idea to varnish the effect, not only to protect the decoration, but to ensure the tray can be easily cleaned and spills swiftly wiped away.

Colourwashing and stamping
The loose application of paint around the rim and in the centre of this tray is constrained by the contrastingly sharp thin line in the lilac area. The colours contrast too; warm brown, blue and orange dots stamped against cool lilac and mauve.

Decoupage and hand-painting
All manner of fish swim busily across this trough-like tray, making a motley arrangement of shapes. Working with a theme will give your work coherence, and arranging your motifs at different angles on a surface will ensure the design is never dull.

Lining with pearlized paint

A pretty decorative tray with rococo-style moulding needs an appropriate treatment. These pearly blue lines are soft but flashy, while the latticework decoration is a motif found on a lot of classically painted furniture.

Masking fluid

A single motif on a tray can look stunning, especially when it is large and comical like this one. This is an old metal tray that has been transformed into a contemporary object, ready to make you smile every time it is used.

Sponging and metal leaf

This wooden tray looks like an impressionist painting in a richly gilded frame. The whole picture has been built up by sponging terracottas and mauves with blues and greens, while the gold and terracotta 'frame' perfectly encases the whole scene.

Crackle varnish

The crazed effect produced by crackle varnish looks like the finish on an old china plate, aged by years of use and contact with hot water. Use the crackle varnish unevenly over a contemporary colour however, and the effect is modern and fresh.

Roller stencilling

On this tray, the play of the earthy brown woodgrain with the green and russet oak leaves puts one in mind of a forest walk. There is a good contrast between the textured and almost transparent base and the solid quality of the leaves.

Candlesticks

CANDLES CAN BE a necessity or an indulgence, and the candlesticks we use to hold them can be symbolic of luxurious grandeur, or have a nostalgic quality, recollecting a more simple life. Always remember to varnish a painted candlestick, strengthening its decoration to withstand hot melted wax. The traditional shape of the obelisk has a number of flat surfaces which are great to decorate and provide the furniture painter with the perfect opportunity to use an elegant finish.

Crackleglaze
The pale, bluish-green effect painted on to this candlestick is reminiscent of verdigris. In places the thick top coat paint has trickled into rivulets.

Metal leaf
By gilding just a few areas of this black-painted candlestick, a flawless elegance is achieved. Metal leaf was used because it is that little bit shinier than bronze powders or metallic paint.

Red tortoiseshell
The long, gently tapered shape of this candlestick requires a suitably elegant finish, and this red tortoiseshell effect has a richness and solidity that makes it the ideal decoration.

Distressing with wax
A rustic, aged finish seemed perfect for this sturdy old wooden candleholder. The off-white paint looks like old whitewash that has worn away with time.

Marble effect
Marbling an object gives it weight and presence, and is a technique that is best suited to a classical piece, like this obelisk. It is useful to study real marble and its colours before attempting to paint it.

Metallic effects
The combination of gold and black is very sophisticated and has really smartened up these small candleholders. The freehand designs are small and simple, yet classical in origin.

Sponging on
The hard, black, polished surface of granite, imitated with glaze and a sponge, makes a smart finish for a candlestick. The colours you use can be varied so that lighter greys, blues and earthy reds and ochres are introduced.

Decorative graining
The classic shape of
the obelisk has been
given a contemporary,
offbeat look by using a
graining roller, but not
conventional
woodgrain colours.

Distressed gilding
This candlestick, large
enough to adorn a
baronial hall, needs a
strong, powerful finish
to match its presence.
Metal leaf alone would
be too overpowering,
but lightly distressing
the leaf creates the
perfect finish.

KEY TO THE TECHNIQUES

Red tortoiseshell
The candlestick
was painted in a
tortoiseshell
effect (see p. 85)
using light and
dark tones of
crimson red.

**Distressing
with wax**
An off-white **matt**
paint (see p. 62)
was **distressed
with wax** (see p.
118) using **clear
wax** (see p. 124).

Marble effect
A **marble** effect
(see p. 84) was
painted using
ochres, grey-
browns and white.
Matt ochre paint
(see p. 62) covers
the mouldings.

Metallic effects
Over a **matt**
black base (see
p. 62), **freehand
motifs** (see
pp. 97–98) were
applied in gold
metallic paint
(see p. 109).

Sponging on
Over a black **mid-
sheen/semi-
gloss** base (see
p. 62), light grey,
mid-grey and
white were
sponged on
(see p. 75).

Over a **mid-
sheen/semi-
gloss** base (see
p. 62), **bronze
powders** (see
p. 108) were
applied to sized
freehand motifs
(see pp. 97–98).

Crackleglaze
A diluted grey-
green top coat
was used over a
light brown base
coat with
crackleglaze
medium (see p.
121) in between.

Metal leaf
Dutch **metal leaf**
(see pp. 104–105)
was applied to
the raised areas
over a black **mid-
sheen/semi-
gloss** base
(see p. 62),

**Distressed
gilding**
Over a matt
terracotta base
(see p. 62) Dutch
metal leaf was
distressed
(see p. 106).

**Decorative
graining**
Over a mid-green
base, dark green
glaze was
grained (see
pp. 86–87) and
sponged on (see
p. 75) in places.

Bowls

B OWLS ARE GREAT FUN to paint; because they are small
they can be quickly decorated, yet they also offer two
distinct surfaces, the inside and outside, which can be
treated differently. Painted bowls are best used for decoration
since the paintwork will not withstand lots of washing.

KEY TO THE TECHNIQUES

Gilded glass
On these three glass bowls the leaf has been applied from the inside
and the paint applied over the top, also on the inside. The decoration is
then viewed from the outside.
Pearlized paint: copper **metal leaf** (see pp. 104–105) was applied in
patches and lines scored through it with a pencil. Blue **pearlized paint**
(see p. 73) was gently and unevenly applied and covered with a coat of
matt dark blue paint (see p. 62).
Matt paint: torn pieces of copper, Dutch metal and aluminium **metal
leaf** (see pp. 104–105) were applied to the inside of the bowl and **matt**
red paint (see p. 62) gently applied over the top.
Spray paint: torn pieces of copper, Dutch metal and aluminium **metal
leaf** (see pp. 104–105) were applied to the inside of the bowl and
covered with green then blue **spray paint** (see p. 63).

Glossy glaze paints
The bowl was painted using
turquoise and green **glossy
glaze paints** (see p. 72). A fish
motif was **decoupaged** (see
pp. 110–111) in the centre.

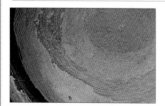

Wax resist
Clear **wax** (see pp. 124–125)
was applied in spots and painted
over in blue and green. Wax was
rubbed in again, removing the
paint where the original wax was.

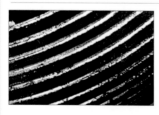

Metal leaf
Over a **matt** blue base (see p. 62)
aluminium **metal leaf** (see
pp. 104–105) was applied in the
grooves, using a small brush to
help push the leaf in.

Distressing and combing
Grey paint was **distressed
with wax** (see p. 118) all over.
Black **glossy glaze paint** (see
p. 72) was **combed** (see p. 79)
in the central area.

**Gilded glass:
pearlized paint**
An aquatic lustre surrounds
these gilded shapes which
float on an iridescent sea of
blue pearlized paint.

Glossy glaze paints
Empty the contents of this
bowl and find a fat fish
swimming lazily by. The
transparent layers of green
and blue paint make looking
down into this simple wooden
bowl like looking into a pool.

Wax resist
Stripes and spots are the simplest elements of decoration. Here the spots are used in an exuberant way, loosely and without keeping to a rigid pattern. The delicate warmth of the wood is enhanced by using cool blues and greens for a contemporary look.

Gilded glass: spray paint
This glass bowl has been decorated with small torn shapes of copper, Dutch metal and aluminium leaf, giving it a delicate look. The two spray paints used to cover the leaf produce a spattered look when viewed from the outside.

Gilded glass: matt paint
Fragments of metal leaf in different colours have been used to provide both a warm and cool contrast to the red paint behind them, giving a dramatic look to this bowl.

Metal leaf
A terracotta bowl with incised lines in it makes a good starting point for a very simple contemporary effect. The bright shiny aluminium lines contrast sharply with the matt blue and the terracotta inside.

Distressing and combing
The rounded shape of this bowl makes it look like it is made of clay, but is in fact made from wood. Inspired by this idea, the bowl was painted to look like some styles of African bowls, which have incisions made in the clay and are baked to a shiny black finish.

Decorating Techniques

Equipment

IT IS POSSIBLE TO PAINT furniture with the minimum of equipment – just a brush and some paint to begin with. Add some glaze to the paint and some a few tools, like a rag and a sponge, and a whole range of paint effects becomes possible. Even the more specialist materials, such as gilding tools, crackleglaze medium and dragging brushes are readily available from good paint shops, craft supermarkets, by mail order (see p. 127) or from art suppliers. They needn't be expensive either. To begin with, try experimenting with improvised tools from around the home, such as children's glue and scissors for decoupage and an ordinary paintbrush instead of a stencilling brush. However, there are no substitutes for some of the brushes and tools.

Brushes

Although you should always try to buy good quality brushes, it is not advisable to buy highly expensive specialist brushes if they will only be used once. Instead, look for a cheaper alternative. Aim to gather a collection of brushes one by one, rather than buying the whole lot in one go.

Basic brushes

Everyday, flat-ended paintbrushes are used for applying paint and glaze, but if you are planning on painting a lot of furniture you may want to invest in an oval-shaped, continental-style brush which holds a lot of paint or glaze. Always buy good quality brushes which are long-lasting and do not shed hairs and choose a size appropriate to your task.

5cm (2in) flat-ended paintbrush

2.5cm (1in) flat-ended paintbrush

Round-ended oval brush

Flat-ended oval brush

Stippling and dragging brushes

The stippling brush lifts off glaze to reveal tiny dots of base colour, while the dragging brush produces a pattern of broken stripes. Do not invest in professional-quality brushes unless you plan to use them a lot, instead use the student-quality brushes available from good paint suppliers. Stippling brushes come in a variety of sizes so buy one in a size that is appropriate to the job in hand.

2.5 x 10cm (1 x 4in) stippling brush

7.5 x 10cm (3 x 4 in) stippling brush

Dragging brush

Rigger and softening brush

These specialist brushes are used when painting faux stone effects. The badger-hair brush is very soft and flexible. It blends glaze colours together and gives a smooth finish. The rigger is a specialist artist's brush used when veining a marble effect.

Rigger

Badger-hair softening brush

Stencil brushes and rollers

Stencil brushes have stiff bristles and are designed to hold a small amount of paint. A small roller is perfect for stencilling.

Roller tray and roller

Stencil brushes

Artists' brushes

Artists' brushes, used for freehand painting, lining and other details, are available in a range of sizes, with a variety of hair and bristle mixes and with different shaped ends.

Pointed artist's brush

Pointed artist's brush

Round-ended artist's brush

Flat-ended artist's brush

Flat-ended artist's brush

Round-ended artist's brush

Gilding

Gilding techniques require little in the way of specialist brushes. You can use an ordinary paintbrush to apply the size, but you will need a soft brush to dab down metal leaf, to smooth it out and help it adhere. Any soft brush will do, but a gilder's mop is specially designed to do the job.

Gilder's mop

Varnish brushes

Using a good quality varnish brush will make the job much easier. Use an acrylic-fibre brush with water-based varnishes and a natural-fibre brush with oil-based varnishes.

Acrylic-fibre varnish brush

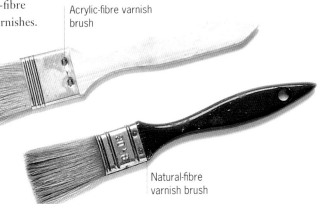

Natural-fibre varnish brush

Paints and colouring mediums

In this book we have chosen to only use water-based decorators' paints because they mix with water-based glaze, can be diluted with water and are easy to use. Other colouring mediums used on the furniture in this book include coloured inks, spray paints and artists' paints, both oil and acrylic.

Matt paint
A matt paint has a completely flat finish, with no shine. Water-based matt paints – such as matt emulsion/latex or specialist decorator's paint – are absorbent and good for decorative work such as stencilling, stamping, ageing techniques and colouring water-based glaze. They can also be diluted with water for freehand painting.

Mid-sheen/semi-gloss paint
A water-based mid-sheen/semi-gloss paint is between matt and glossy in texture. There are various makes on the market, including satin and silk. Because it has a slightly shiny finish it is good on objects that require frequent cleaning and because it is not too absorbent it is excellent as a base coat to water-based glazes.

Pearlized paint
This reflective water-based paint produces a luminescent, pearlized effect which takes on different characteristics depending on the base colour.

Glossy glaze paint
This water-based paint is available from specialist paint suppliers or can be bought mail order (see p. 127). It has a translucent glossy finish and is used for its wonderful shine. A similar effect can be achieved using acrylic gloss paint thinned with water and finished with a gloss varnish.

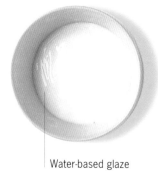

Water-based glaze

Water-based paint

Glaze
Water-based glaze is a slow-drying, colourless, transparent medium used for most paint effects. It can be coloured using any water-based paint or with powder pigments. The more paint added the deeper the colour will be and the quicker the glaze will dry.

Powder pigments
Powder pigments are colour in their purest form and should be used sparingly. They can be used to colour glaze, varnish or wax.

Brown pigment

Red pigment

Yellow pigment

Other paints

Spray paints – including the kind used on cars – are great for stencilling and painting glass. Artists' oil paints are used in ageing techniques and artists' acrylics can be used for freehand painting or colouring glaze.

Spray paint

Artist's oil paint

Artist's acrylic paint

Inks and masking fluid

Waterproof drawing inks or writing inks are used with mapping pens or artists' brushes to produce an opaque covering. Masking fluid dries to a rubbery consistency that rejects any decoration applied over the top.

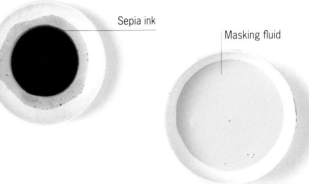

Indian ink

Sepia ink

Masking fluid

General equipment

There are a number of useful decorating tools that you will find yourself constantly using for a range of different tasks and techniques. Many of these items can already be found around the home, others will need to be bought specially; once invested in, however, they will no doubt be put to good use again and again.

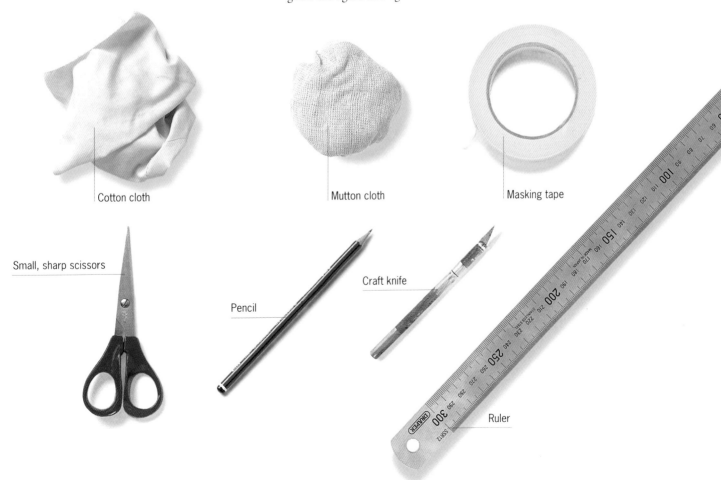

Cotton cloth

Mutton cloth

Masking tape

Small, sharp scissors

Pencil

Craft knife

Ruler

Specific equipment

Some of the equipment needed for specific techniques can be found in the home or locally – sponges, polystyrene, wrapping paper, glue, tracing paper – while other materials need to be sought out from good paint suppliers, specialist art suppliers or by mail order (see p. 127).

Paint effects

A natural sponge makes a wonderfully textured mark and can be used to either apply glaze or dab it off. Graining rollers and combs were originally used to imitate woodgrains but are now more often used to create decorative effects in their own right.

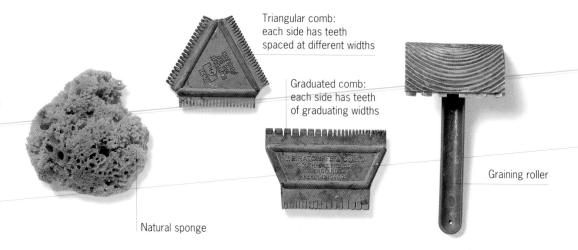

Triangular comb: each side has teeth spaced at different widths

Graduated comb: each side has teeth of graduating widths

Graining roller

Natural sponge

Stencilling and stamping

When making your own stencils it is advisable to buy a heat knife to cut cleanly through acetate. When cutting with a craft knife, however, you must do so over a self-healing cutting mat. Sponges and polystyrene make great stamping materials.

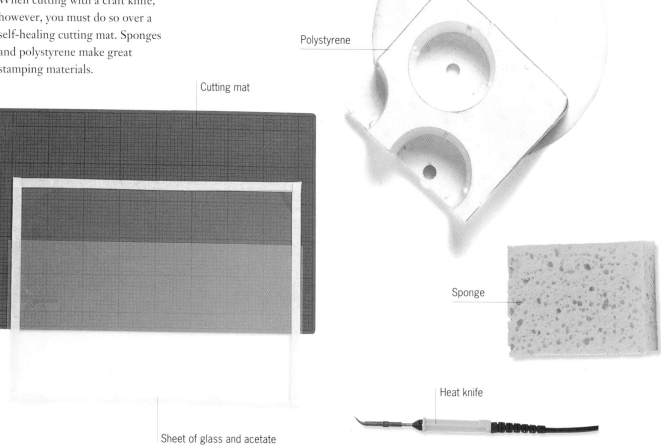

Cutting mat

Polystyrene

Sponge

Heat knife

Sheet of glass and acetate

Gilding

Dutch metal (imitation gold), aluminium (imitation silver) and copper loose metal leaf is adhered to any smooth surface using a special glue called gold size. Dusting your hands with French chalk prevents the delicate leaf sticking to your fingers. Bronze powders are fine metallic powders, also adhered using gold size.

Water-based gold size

Dutch metal leaf

Rich pale gold

Pale gold

Antique copper

Fire copper

Copper

Light gold

Medium gold

French chalk

Decoupage

As well as some sharp scissors, plenty of varnish and your choice of paper, you will also need a good quality glue, one that is not too thick and does not dry too quickly. Paper glue, white wood glue and a specialist starch glue are the best choices.

Wrapping paper

Wood-effect papers

Plain papers

Glue

Source books

Freehand painting

By using tracing paper you do not need
to be an accomplished artist to transfer
an illustration on to furniture and fill it
in with paint. If you prefer to work with
ink, then you will need a mapping pen
which is dipped into the ink.

Image and
tracing paper

Mapping pen

Ageing techniques

Crackle varnish and crackleglaze
are specialist mediums which
produce crazed effects. The
crackle varnish is a two-part
medium which, as it dries, forms
into a network of cracks, while
crackleglaze is applied between
two coats of paint and recreates
the effect of peeling paint.

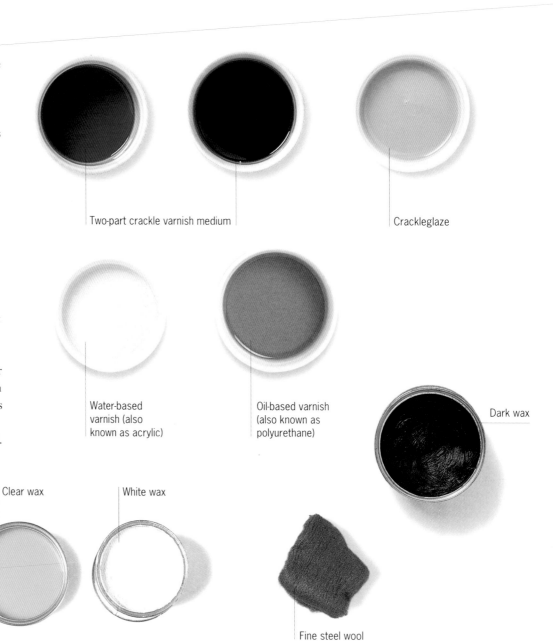

Two-part crackle varnish medium

Crackleglaze

Varnish and wax

The two main types of varnish
are water-based and oil-based.
Oil-based varnishes have a slight
yellowed look when dry, while
water-based varnishes dry clear.
The two types of clear wax (clear
and neutral) have the same finish
and there are a number of shades
of dark wax for different effects.
Apply waxes with fine steel wool.

Water-based
varnish (also
known as acrylic)

Oil-based varnish
(also known as
polyurethane)

Dark wax

Neutral wax

Clear wax

White wax

Fine steel wool

Preparing surfaces

Preparing surfaces properly before painting is very important. Use a commercial paint stripper on old paint and varnish, remembering to wear protective gloves. A wax remover cleans away old wax and dirt and a rust inhibitor is essential on metal. Some deeply grained woods may need to be filled, while absorbent wood surfaces can be sealed using commercial sanding sealer. Different grades of sandpaper are used for different jobs and tack cloth is a useful material for removing dust after sanding.

Paint stripper

Coarse steel wool

Protective gloves

Wire brush

Wax remover

Wood filler

Rust inhibitor

Trowel

Sanding sealer

Tack cloth

Mixed sandpapers and sanding block

Preparing Surfaces

THIS ESSENTIAL PART of the furniture painting process is the least fun. However, attention must be paid to preparing your surfaces to ensure that your chosen decoration both looks good and lasts. Brand new objects need little preparation; rough wood will need sanding and a coat of paint or sanding sealer may be required to seal the surface, but older objects, on the other hand, are bound to need some work.

To ensure that new paint adheres to a surface, any old paint, especially glossy oil-based paints and varnishes, must be removed.

Paint will also not adhere if applied to a greasy or waxy surface, but a commercial wax remover will sort this problem out in no time.

Rust on metal can be quickly remedied, and if your old veneers have become unstuck you can probably reglue them using a domestic iron. Some techniques demand a really smooth surface so the well-pronounced grain of certain woods will need to be treated with a grain filler.

Although it may all sound just a little tiresome, it really is well worth it in the long run.

Removing paint and varnish

Old coats of varnish or paint on a surface will become unstable if they are painted over. Therefore, it is necessary to remove them with a commercial paint stripper before starting a new decoration.

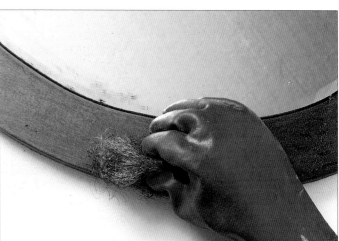

1 Commercial paint stripper is caustic and should be used with care; always wear protective gloves when handling it. Using an old paintbrush, apply a generous amount of paint stripper to the surface. Leave the stripper on until the old coat of paint or varnish begins to bubble.

2 Rub coarse steel wool all over the surface to remove the newly softened paint or varnish.

3 If necessary, repeat the process with a second coat of paint stripper, using an old toothbrush to ensure the stripper gets into the crevices of carved or moulded surfaces.

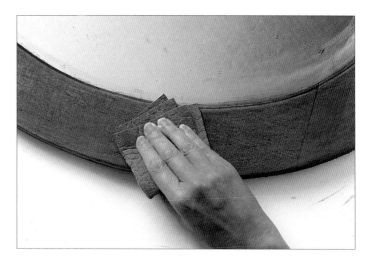

4 Remove excess stripper or particles of paint or varnish using a damp cloth or sponge and the neutralizer recommended by your product.

Removing wax and dirt

Wax and dirt, like old coats of varnish and paint, are likely to interfere with the new decoration, but they can be easily cleaned away using a commercial wax remover.

1 When using a commercial wax remover, work in small sections at a time, since the product dries quite quickly. Soak fine steel wool in the wax remover and rub it into your surface. Do not let the steel wool dry out.

2 While the surface is still wet, wipe off the loosened wax and dirt using a dry, soft cloth. Repeat the process if necessary.

Treating rusty metal

New metal objects do not need any preparation, as long as they have a smooth surface. Old metal, however, should be cleared of existing rust and protected against the formation of new rust.

1 Rub the metal surface vigorously with a wire brush to remove the loose, powdery fragments of old rust.

2 Apply a rust inhibitor all over the surface, following the instructions given by your product. Leave to dry.

3 Cover the surface with a coat of paint designed for use on metal.

Filling wood

If you want to decorate a deeply grained wooden object using a
technique that calls for a smooth surface, such as gilding, you will need
to fill and sand the wood until completely flat.

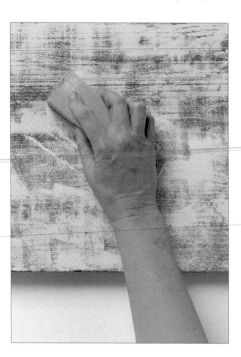

1 Choose a fine filler suitable for use on wood.
Using a palette knife, apply a small amount of
filler at a time, pressing down hard to fill the dents
and smooth the filler. Leave to dry.

2 Rub down the filled surface using some
medium-grade sandpaper wrapped around
a sanding block.

3 Dilute a matt or mid-sheen/semi-gloss paint
(see p. 62) to a ratio of nine parts paint to one
part water and apply evenly all over the surface.

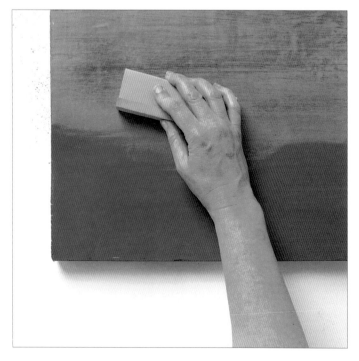

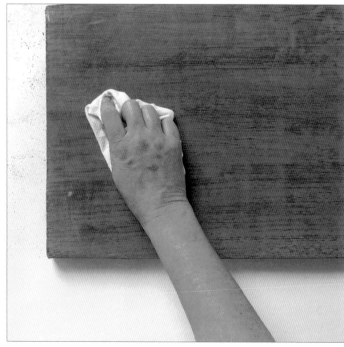

4 Rub the surface down again, this time using fine-grade sandpaper
wrapped around a sanding block.

5 Wipe the surface clean with a soft cloth. Paint the surface again, this time
using undiluted paint and spreading it out well.

Resticking veneers

When working with old pieces of furniture you may come across a veneer that is peeling from the surface. This imperfection can usually be quickly remedied.

1 First test the flexibility of the veneer by pressing down on it. If the veneer cracks under the pressure, you will need to have it professionally filled. If it does not crack, you can remedy the fault yourself.

2 Cover the loose veneer with a sheet of brown paper and press down on it with a hot iron. Keep pressing until the glue beneath heats up and sticks the veneer back together.

Sealing new wood

New wood can be very absorbent, making it difficult to cover with solid colour. To stop new wood soaking up paint or varnish, coat the surface with a commercial sanding sealer.

2 To remove the shine of the sealer and reveal any missed areas, rub down the surface using medium-grade sandpaper wrapped around a wooden block, following the direction of the grain.

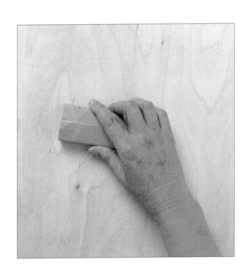

1 Because sanding sealer is colourless, it is necessary to choose a systematic order of work, to avoid missing areas or going over the same area twice. Use a paintbrush to apply the sanding sealer and allow to dry following your product's instructions.

3 Apply a second coat of sealer if necessary. Leave to dry and sand as before.

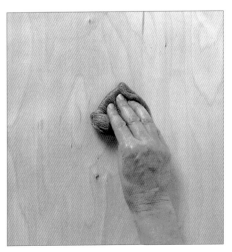

4 To remove excess sanding sealer that has not been absorbed, rub down the surface using fine steel wool.

Simple Paint Finishes

THERE ARE MANY different paints on the market today, with a variety of finishes. Couple these with the different methods of applying paint, and the furniture painter has a range of textures and effects to play with. The first thing to practise before painting furniture is the correct way to apply paint.

It is surprising how many unsatisfactory results are due to applying the paint too thickly. It is also useful to look at some of the new paints on the market – such as pearlized paints and glossy glaze paints – and learn how best to apply them, as well as learning the different ways to apply two or more colours as a base coat.

Applying paint

One thing to remember when applying any kind of paint is not to overload the brush or apply too much paint at one time. The translucent, water-based, glossy glaze paint is excellent for merging colours, but dries in approximately five minutes so you cannot keep working over one application as you can with matt paints. The translucent pearlized paint has a luminescent finish which makes it shiny in some lights and matt in others; the final effect varies depending on the base colour used.

Applying matt or mid-sheen/semi-gloss paint

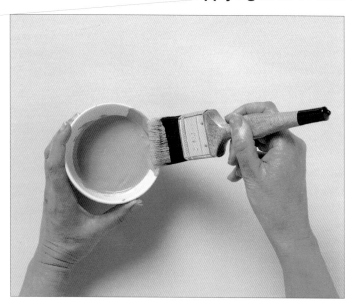

2 Use the full length of the brush to apply the paint, not just the tip. At this stage, the surface should retain a reasonably thick coat of paint.

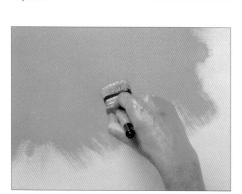

3 To thin the paint, turn the brush at roughly a 90-degree angle to the surface and use the tip to spread the paint over a larger area. Protect if necessary when dry (see pp. 122–125).

1 Aim to immerse about one-third to half the bristles of your paintbrush in the paint. Gently press the brush against the rim of the paint container to remove excess paint.

Applying glossy glaze paint

1 Over a mid-sheen/semi-gloss base (see p. 62), apply a thin layer of glossy glaze paint to part of your object. Leave to dry and apply a second colour, starting on the unpainted section and overlapping part of the first painted colour.

2 Apply more colours as you wish. You can overlap an area that has already been painted twice to make a third colour with even greater depth. If necessary, protect the effect when dry (see pp. 122–125).

Applying pearlized paint

1 First paint your object in matt paint (see p. 62) and leave to dry. Here, a box has been painted in deep blue and deep green. Apply the pearlized paint generously but not thickly.

2 The paint is white when wet but dries to a translucent colour. Although not as slow drying as glaze, this paint can be treated in a similar way to make textured effects (see pp. 74–87). If desired, protect the dried effect (see pp. 122–125).

Dry brush

Pick up a very small amount of matt paint (see p. 62) on a dry brush – choose a colour that is close in tone to the existing painted base. Using only the tip of the brush, paint in straight lines across the surface, releasing just a little paint for a loose striped effect. Protect the dry effect if desired (see pp. 122–125).

Variegated colour

1 For this technique you will need two – or more – matt or mid-sheen/semi-gloss paints. Paint the first colour in an irregular shape, using a generous amount of paint.

2 Use the same brush to apply an equally generous amount of the second colour, also in an irregular shape, and slightly overlapping the still-wet first colour. Use the tip of the brush to blend the two colours together.

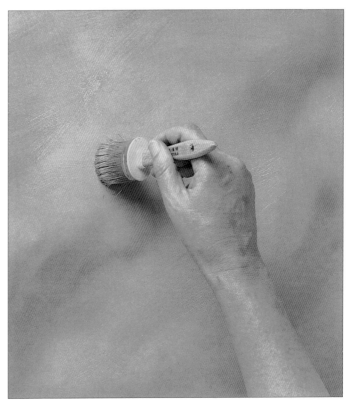

3 Continue making irregular shapes and merging paints across the surface. The change of colour should be soft and subtle and the overall effect is cloudy. Soften the finish by dabbing the surface with the flat end of the brush before the paints dry. Protect the dry finish if necessary (see pp. 122–125).

Paint Effects

ALL PAINT EFFECTS use at least two colours to give a surface a textured look. A solid paint base coat is covered with a translucent, coloured glaze top coat, which can be manipulated with various materials to create all kinds of patterns.

Glaze is a transparent medium which dries slowly. It is coloured with paint or pigment, but remains translucent so the base coat can shine through. Because the medium is slow drying, the painter has time to manipulate the glaze with one of many possible materials, revealing the base coat in places.

A host of different patterns can be created using a range of materials. With rags or soft cloths it is possible to produce a colourwash or ragged effect while sponges can be used to dab glaze off or on. An ordinary paintbrush can be used to create a tartan effect, while specialist brushes like the dragging brush and the stippling brush produce their own unique patterns. A comb and a graining roller can be used in a multitude of ways, and newspaper never produces the same look twice.

More complex patterns can be made using brushes, an eye for detail, some confidence and a little practice. To reproduce effects like a painted sky, a bird's-eye maple woodgrain and painted marble or tortoiseshell it is important to study the real thing. Your interpretation does not have to be an attempt at an exact copy, but it does need to suggest the character of the original.

Although these paint effects have been in use for many years, they are constantly changing, because each generation uses them in new and different ways.

Ragging

Ragging needs no specialist tools, just a paintbrush and a soft cloth. Use a material that contains a lot of cotton, old sheeting for example. If the material has a high nylon content or is shiny then it will not absorb the glaze. You could also try using a cloth with a prominent texture.

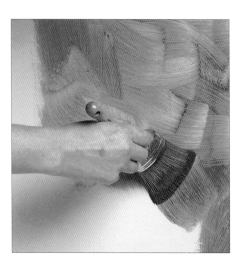

1 Apply a base coat of mid-sheen/semi-gloss paint (see p. 62). Use random brush strokes to apply a coat of coloured glaze (see p. 62). When ragging large pieces of furniture it is a good idea to work in small, manageable-sized sections. Leave a strip of unragged wet glaze at the edge of each section and work back into it when applying the next section of glaze.

2 Dab a crumpled cotton rag into the still-wet glaze to lift it off, revealing the base colour in places. Re-form the rag as it becomes covered with glaze, and replace it when it becomes saturated. Protect the dry effect with varnish or wax if desired (see pp. 122–125).

RAGGING WITH OTHER MATERIALS

A variety of interesting effects can be achieved by using different materials when ragging. Try crumpling up a plastic bag, some paper towel or some cling film and using it in the same way as a rag, dabbing it over a wet glaze coat and revealing the base coat in places. The plastics will produce a strong pattern that is more clearly defined than ragging, while a paper towel gives a softer, spotted finish. Replace both materials frequently as they become covered or saturated with glaze.

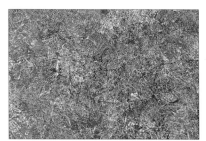

Ragging with plastic

Ragging with paper towel

Sponging on

Natural marine sponges have an interesting texture which produces an
irregular pattern when used to apply coloured glaze. Different sponges give
different effects, so try to use one sponge for one project.

1 Apply a mid-sheen/semi-gloss base coat to the surface, then pour your coloured glaze (see p. 62) into a paint tray. Dip a damp sponge into the glaze and dab it lightly on the surface. Vary the pressure you exert on the sponge to add variety to the effect and prevent it becoming regimented.

2 When the first layer of sponging is dry you can sponge the surface again using a different coloured glaze. Because the previous coat is dry any mistakes can be easily wiped clean. Vary the overall effect by leaving different-sized gaps between sponge prints, and adding a third layer in a different colour. Protect the finish if necessary when dry (see pp. 122–125).

Sponging off

In this technique a dampened natural marine sponge is used to lift coloured glaze from the surface,
producing an informal patterned effect. The sponge should not be too wet or too dry; if it is too wet it
will leave drips on the surface, if too dry it will be difficult to lift the glaze.

1 Over a mid-sheen/semi-gloss base coat paint on the coloured glaze (see p. 62) using random brush strokes, making sure the surface is well covered. When sponging large pieces of furniture work in small, manageable sections. Leave a strip of wet unsponged glaze at the edge of each section and work back into this strip when applying glaze to the next section.

2 Take a damp sponge and dab it over the surface removing some of the still-wet glaze and revealing the base colour in places. Remember to rinse the sponge out in clean water before it becomes saturated and starts putting glaze back on to the surface rather than removing it. Protect the finished effect if desired when dry (see pp. 122–125).

Colourwashing

This technique can be carried out on uneven surfaces since it will disguise many imperfections. The trick to successful colourwashing is to wait until the glaze has begun to dry before wiping it off. If the glaze is too wet you will remove too much, leaving a coarse effect, but when it has dried a little you can apply varying amounts of pressure to achieve a soft, diverse finish.

1 Over a mid-sheen/semi-gloss base coat apply a coat of coloured glaze (see p. 62) using criss-cross brush strokes. When colourwashing large pieces of furniture work in small, manageable sections. Leave a strip of wet, uncolourwashed glaze at the edge of each section to work back into it when applying glaze to next section.

2 As the top coat begins to dry, take a crumpled soft cloth and rub it into the glaze using sweeping strokes of different lengths and working in all directions. Apply different degrees of pressure to the cloth to vary the effect, but do not press so hard that you completely remove the glaze. When the cloth becomes saturated refold it or use a fresh piece. Protect the finished effect if necessary (see pp. 122–125).

COLOURWASHING WITH BRUSHES

Instead of a soft cloth, brushes can be used to remove glaze for different colourwash effects. Here, a hard-bristled decorator's brush was used for a powerful, coarse effect that clearly reveals the marks of the bristles.

A soft wallpaper brush was used to remove the glaze in this example. Although the effect is still harsher than when using a soft cloth, the brushmarks are less distinct than if a hard brush had been used.

Stippling

The specialist stippling brush used for this technique is available in a
range of sizes, so choose a size that is appropriate to the area you are
decorating. Use this technique only on a very smooth object since the
effect shows up any bumps or imperfections in the surface.

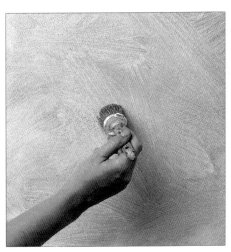

1 Over a base coat of mid-sheen/semi-gloss paint brush on the coloured glaze (see p. 62) in all directions, spreading it out thinly. When stippling large pieces of furniture, work in manageable-sized sections. Leave a strip of unstippled wet glaze at the edge of each section to work back into.

2 Use the tip of the brush to work back over the glaze, smoothing it out and removing any visible brushmarks.

3 Firmly dab the flat surface of the stippling brush into the still-wet glaze, breaking it up and revealing the base colour in tiny dots. Repeat the stippling action across the surface, overlapping previously stippled areas. As the stippling brush becomes saturated with glaze, gently wipe it clean with a dry cloth.

STIPPLING WITH OTHER BRUSHES

To produce a similar yet less ordered finish, try stippling glaze using any brush with short, rigid bristles, such as the dustpan brush used here. The bristles on a dustpan brush are clustered together in small groups, a characteristic which leaves a noticeable pattern in the glaze.

Finished effect
It is only apparent that this delicate and sophisticated finish is made up of tiny dots on close inspection. The ideal stippled finish should be evenly and finely speckled. To protect the decoration use a varnish or wax (see pp. 122–125).

Dragging

This technique uses a specialist dragging brush which makes
variegated stripes in the glaze. You can vary the pressure you apply
with the dragging brush to give subtle or strident effects.

1 Working over a mid-sheen/semi-gloss base coat, paint on the coloured
glaze (see p. 62) in straight lines and spread it out evenly. When dragging
a large item apply the glaze in small sections of horizontal or vertical strips.
Leave a wet edge of undragged glaze to work the next strip of glaze into.

2 Draw a dragging brush through the still-wet glaze holding the brush
almost parallel to the surface. Work back and forth across the surface to
give a striped finish, using different degrees of pressure on the brush to vary
the effect. Wipe away the excess glaze from a saturated brush with a clean,
dry cloth. Protect the finished effect when dry if necessary (see pp. 122–125).

DRAGGING WITH A CLOTH

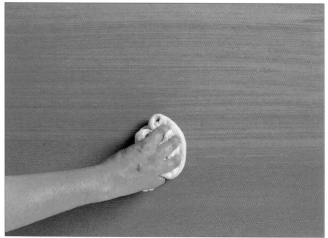

1 To produce a softer finish that has a slightly less distinct striped
pattern than traditional dragging, try dragging with a soft cloth. Apply
the coloured glaze in straight lines over a mid-sheen/semi-gloss base
coat and spread it out evenly as in Step 1 of Dragging (above).

2 Take a crumpled up soft cloth and drag it across the surface in a
straight line, trying not to stop in the middle. To help keep the lines
straight, concentrate on a straight edge of the surface and always drag
in the same direction.

Combing

The specialist comb was originally developed – and is still used – for imitating woodgrains, but it can also be put to good use as a decorative tool in its own right. Commercial combs can be bought with teeth of varying widths and are used to create a vast range of effects including stripes, checks and wavy lines. It is important that you remember not to apply the coloured glaze too thickly as this will result in a three-dimensional ridged effect.

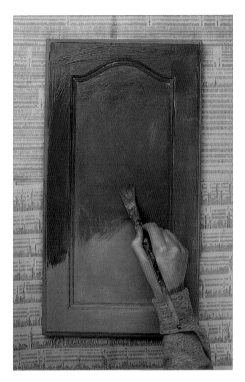

1 Over a mid-sheen/semi-gloss base coat, paint on the coloured glaze (see p. 62), brushing it out thinly and evenly. If combing a large piece of furniture apply the glaze in small, manageable sections. Leave a strip of wet uncombed glaze at the edge of each section to work back into when applying glaze to the next section.

2 Hold the comb firmly and with the teeth slanted upward – here the thickest width of a triangular comb is being used – and pull it through the glaze from top to bottom. Use the comb in the same way to make a horizontal pattern. Wipe excess glaze from the comb as you work.

3 For an undulating, almost three-dimensional effect, pull the comb through the glaze using a wavy hand movement, still working from top to bottom. To vary the design, comb through the glaze a second time. Varnish or wax if desired when dry (see pp. 122–125).

Finished effect

A wonderful range of patterns can be produced by combing. The size of the teeth and the direction and design of the strokes can be varied to create numerous combinations.

Frottage

When a sheet of newspaper is rubbed into still-wet dilute paint it produces an irregular pattern, highlighted by small lines. You can vary the pressure you apply when rubbing the newspaper to control the amount of paint that is removed, and therefore the end result.

1 Dilute a matt or mid-sheen/semi-gloss paint (see p. 62) to a ratio of two parts paint to one part water. Apply the mixture generously to the surface in an area that is slightly larger than a sheet of newspaper.

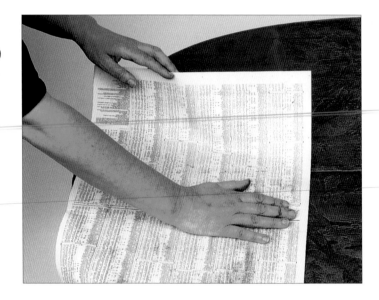

2 Lay a clean sheet of newspaper over the wet paint, leaving a wet edge of dilute paint not covered by paper. Smooth your hands over the newspaper without applying too much pressure in one single area. Carefully and quickly, peel off the sheet of paper. Apply the diluted paint to the next section, working back into the previous wet edge, and repeat the process with a fresh sheet of newspaper each time.

USING OTHER MATERIALS

Crumpled tissue paper and strips of an absorbent fabric such as cotton can also be rubbed over a layer of diluted paint to give variation to the traditional frottage technique. The tissue paper produces a smaller, more even pattern than newspaper, while fabric gives a looser, less grainy effect.

Frottage with tissue paper

Frottage with fabric

Finished effect

The newspaper absorbs more paint in some areas than in others, leaving a random textured pattern. A unique effect is achieved with each fresh sheet of newspaper. Protect the finish when dry if desired (see pp. 122–125).

Painting tartan

Coloured glaze can be used to paint an effect similar to tartan fabric. Pulling a brush through the translucent glaze reveals the colour underneath, producing a two-tone effect reminiscent of fabric weave. You can make your tartan as realistic or as stylized as you want, and you may decide to finish the effect by adding a few freehand lines (see pp. 100–101).

1 Paint all over your surface in a dark or light mid-sheen/semi-gloss paint (see p. 62). When the paint is dry, apply a coloured glaze (see p. 62) in vertical stripes.

2 Pull a dry bristle brush through the still-wet glaze, partly revealing the colour underneath. Leave to dry for about 15 minutes.

3 Take a second coloured glaze and apply it in horizontal stripes. Pull through the still-wet glaze with a dry brush as before. To achieve a realistic tartan effect you may want to test your choice of colours on paper first, since trying to remove an unwanted glaze colour from your object will dislodge the base coat. When thoroughly dry, varnish or wax the final effect for protection (see pp. 122–125).

COMBED TARTAN

Instead of dragging a paintbrush through glaze, another effective way of reproducing a tartan look is by combing through glaze (see p. 79). By using combs of different sizes and graduated combs you can imitate the soft movement of the tartan weave, and freehand lines painted over the top only add to the authenticity. You don't need to worry about keeping the combing and freehand painting completely straight either, since wobbly lines give a more natural, fabric feel.

Painting skies

The principal of painting an effective sky using water-based glazes is based around arcs or circles of light and dark blue. If you look at a real sky you will see the blue is deepest at the highest point and gets lighter as the sky meets the earth. On a vertical plane, such as a cupboard door, this effect is recreated using as many as six tones of blue glaze, applied in sweeping arcs working with the darkest at the top, down to the lightest at the bottom. On a horizontal plane, such as the tray here, arcs of different-toned blues face each other to make a circle, again with the darkest at the top.

1 Apply two coats of white mid-sheen/semi-gloss paint (see p. 62) to the surface, sanding each coat to ensure no brush strokes are visible. Mix a light blue glaze (see p. 62) and apply it to the base of the surface. Work in an arc from the base to the centre of the surface and fill in the gap with ever decreasing arc shapes.

2 Mix a darker blue glaze and apply it to the top of the surface in the same way as before, using arc shapes from the top to the centre. When working on a vertical plane start with a dark blue glaze at the top and work down in arcs of gradually lightening blues.

3 Blend the colours together by wiping over the glazes with the tip of a paintbrush. Use a clean cloth to remove excess glaze from the brush as you work.

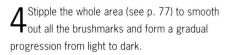

4 Stipple the whole area (see p. 77) to smooth out all the brushmarks and form a gradual progression from light to dark.

5 To make clouds, wipe a cloth into the still-wet glaze in the darker area to reveal the white paint underneath. Wrap a finger or thumb in the cloth and twist your hand to make small and large cloud shapes.

6 On the lighter areas at the base of the surface use the cloth to make long, thin, horizontal lines of cloud. Try to keep the effect light, natural and not too rigid. Leave to dry before protecting with varnish or wax (see pp. 122–125).

Bird's-eye maple graining

Imitating woodgrain is not as difficult as it sounds, and this technique uses no specialist equipment. The secret of effective woodgraining lies in the choice of colour: a thorough examination of real wood will prove invaluable. Here, the technique is worked over a pale wood background but a mid-sheen/semi-gloss paint (see p. 62) in an appropriate colour should be applied over a previously painted background.

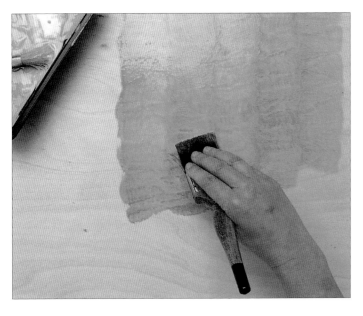

2 Take a clean, flat-ended brush and dab it into the areas where the glaze is wettest and thickest, creating more texture.

1 Load a flat-ended paintbrush with coloured glaze (see p. 62) and pull the brush down the surface, wiggling and angling it as you go. Apply more pressure to the bristles at random intervals to produce darker patches.

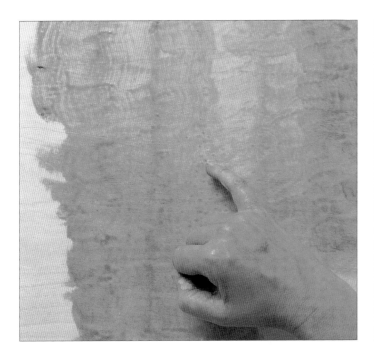

3 Dab the end of your little finger into the areas of the surface where the glaze is still thickest, to make small dots, imitating the 'bird's eyes' which give this wood its name.

Finished effect

In imitation of actual bird's-eye maple, this finish combines light and dark patches of colour, grain lines and bird's eyes. The application of a mid-sheen/semi-gloss varnish (see pp. 122–123) to the dry effect will not only protect it but also help to enhance the feel of real wood.

Painting marble

Before imitating marble, it is important to decide which colours you
want to use. Do this by referring to real marble, which comes in a wide
range of colours and pattern variations.

 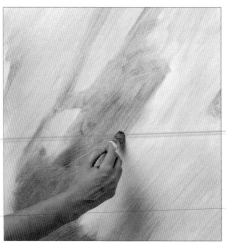 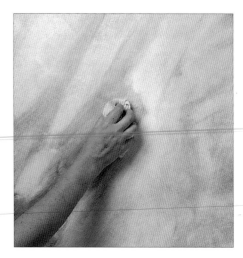

1 Apply a mid-sheen/semi-gloss (see p. 62) base coat in a light colour. Mix three glazes (see p. 62) in three tones of a single colour – light, mid-tone and dark. Apply the lightest glaze colour to the surface in diagonal strokes, varying the angle of the brush.

2 Apply the mid-tone glaze, also using diagonal strokes, but only in irregular patches over the first glaze coat. Then lay on the darkest glaze colour, also in irregular patches and using diagonal strokes. Avoid creating parallel diagonal lines by slightly varying the angle of your brush.

3 While the glaze is still wet, soften the overall effect by dabbing the surface with a smooth pad of mutton cloth. Treat the light and dark areas separately, starting with the lightest, to keep them well defined.

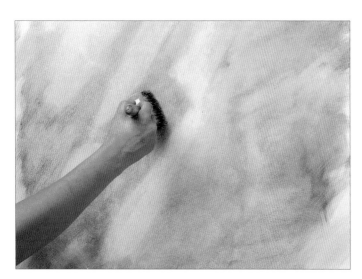

4 While the glaze is still wet, brush all over the surface using a softening brush to remove the mutton cloth marks. To achieve a smooth effect without visible brushmarks, hold the brush at right angles to the surface and move it from side to side, letting the movement come from your arm, not your wrist. If you are happy with the effect at this stage you can finish it, when dry, with a coat of gloss varnish (see pp. 122–123), or go on to further enhance the marble with veining.

5 Slightly thin some decorator's or artist's acrylic paint (see pp. 62–63) in a colour that is a little darker than your darkest glaze colour. Dip an artist's brush into the paint and use it to outline the darker patches and create veins of various thicknesses. Allow the brush to move loosely in your hand, rather than holding it rigidly like a pencil. Always vein in a diagonal direction but avoid creating parallel lines, broken lines or crossing lines. Refer to examples of real marble to help you achieve realistic results.

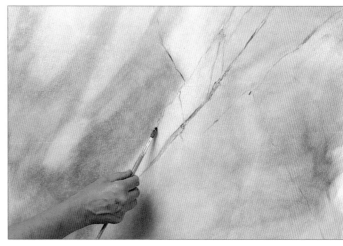

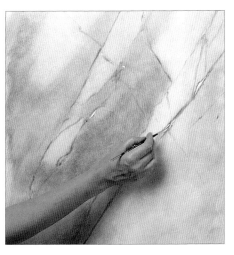

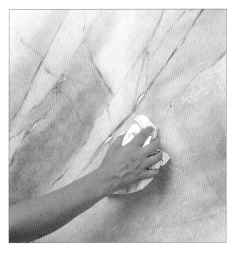

6 Brush the softening brush over the veins to gently blend them into the background. Again, let the movement of the brush come from your arm and not your wrist.

7 To lighten very thick areas of painted veins, dip a specialist rigger brush in some water and brush it into the chosen area while the paint is still wet. This action will remove the paint and glaze to reveal the white base coat, forming an 'island' within the vein.

8 Dab a soft cotton cloth into the veins to soften them further and break up the veining slightly. When dry, apply a coat of gloss varnish which will protect the decoration and give it the authentic look and feel of cold stone.

Painting tortoiseshell

Crafters have been imitating tortoiseshell since the 17th century, not only on small objects like frames and boxes, but also for large pieces of furniture such as cabinets and tables.

1 This technique can be carried out on a mid-sheen/semi-gloss, yellow-painted base (see p. 62) or, as here, on a metal leaf base (see pp. 104–105). Coat the base with a layer of uncoloured glaze (see p. 62) using diagonal strokes. Mix two coloured glazes in shades similar to burnt umber and burnt sienna.

2 Paint small diagonal patches of the first colour on to the previously glazed surface using a soft brush. Slightly vary the size and direction of each patch to avoid a regimented look. Do the same with the second coloured glaze.

3 Using the tip of a softening brush, blend the colours into the uncoloured glaze coat. Work first in the direction of the marks and then in the opposite direction, to produce a soft look without brushmarks. A coat of gloss varnish (see pp. 122–123) will protect the effect and give it an authentic tortoiseshell look and feel.

Using a graining roller

When combined with combing techniques (see p. 79), the specialist
graining roller can produce a reasonably realistic look of wood, but the
pattern it creates when rocked through coloured glaze is equally
effective as a decorative technique used with a variety of colours.

1 Over a mid-sheen/semi-gloss base apply a thin layer of coloured glaze (see p. 62) painting it on in one direction.

2 Use a soft cloth to wipe over the glaze until only a very fine layer remains on the surface; a thick glaze coat will produce a ridged effect.

3 Place the graining roller in position, holding it so that about one-tenth of the arched roller head touches the surface. Using both hands and pressing firmly, pull the graining roller along the surface, gently rocking the roller head as you pull. Continue in strips across the surface. Try to vary the distances you rock the roller through, for instance you could cover the whole width of the surface with just one rocking motion, to produce a long and narrow graining circle.

4 As you work, remember to keep wiping excess glaze from the roller head with a cloth.

5 To obtain a very soft look, gently brush over the grained lines using a dragging brush. Let the glaze dry a little before you do this, if it is still too wet you will obliterate the graining lines completely.

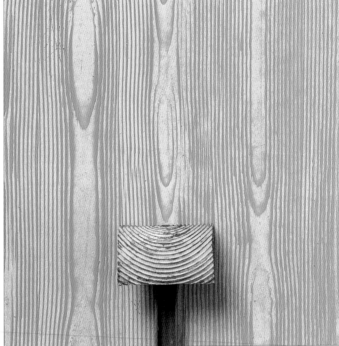

Finished effect

The graining roller has a removable head which can be used to make two different grains. Here the head was used in the 'oak' position, with the arches pointing down. This position produces a wide, open grain effect. Protect the dry finish with varnish or wax if necessary (see pp. 122–125).

Finished effect

Here the head has been used in the 'pine' position, with the arches pointing upwards. This position produces a fine, slim grain effect. Protect the finished effect, when dry, with a coat of varnish or wax if necessary (see p. 122–125).

COMMON MISTAKES

Using the right consistency of glaze is essential if this effect is to be successful, so it is a good idea to practise on a spare surface first if possible. Here are examples of two of the most common mistakes made when using a graining roller. If there is too much glaze on the surface the roller will leave very indistinct graining marks. If too little glaze is left then it will be very difficult to make a mark at all.

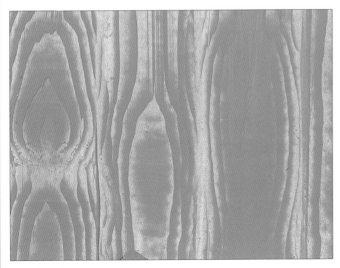

Glaze layer too heavy

Glaze layer too thin

Stencilling and Stamping

STENCILS AND STAMPS allow you to produce unique, customized patterns, and the marvellous thing about them is their flexibility. They can be applied singly, in rows or in groups, used upside down or on an angle. They can be repeated at equal intervals, or positioned randomly, overlapping previous prints occasionally, and they can be applied using as few or as many colours as you like. In fact a stamped or stencilled design can be as varied as patterns on fabric.

Both stencils and stamps can be bought ready-cut, but it is far more fulfilling, and not terribly difficult, to make your own.

The usual definition of stencilling is the application of paint through a shaped hole cut into card or acetate. The opposite effect can be achieved by reverse stencilling. Here the cut shape – a card stencil is necessary for this effect – blocks out the paint which is applied around its edges, leaving a silhouette effect.

Using different methods for applying paint to a stencil will affect the final look. For a country-style, folk-painted look, application with a stencil brush is most appropriate, but, for a clean print of an intricate design, spray paints can be very good. For a more abstract, contemporary look, try using rollers.

Stamps may not always be quite as flexible as stencils, but they are blissfully easy to make and use. On the simplest level household objects such as sponges, paper cups and cardboard can be used to print textured effects, while actual designs can be cut out of polystyrene blocks.

Stencilling with spray paints is a reasonably new innovation, but one that gives a traditional technique a contemporary edge.

Cutting stencils with a heat knife

The heat knife is used to cut acetate stencils, and it is quick and easy to use. However, care should be taken when using this equipment as it does get extremely hot.

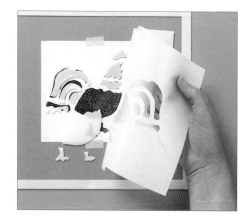

1 Photocopy a template from a copyright-free book or create your own stencil design on paper. Place a sheet of glass, for example the front of a picture frame which will not be marked by the knife, over the design.

2 Use masking tape to fix a sheet of acetate to the glass. Plug in the heat knife and wait for it to heat up, following the manufacturer's instructions. Trace around the design with the point of the heat knife.

3 Carefully untape and remove the acetate. Gently push out any cut shapes that remain attached to the acetate. The flowing quality of the heat knife means that the finished stencil has lovely smooth edges.

Cutting stencils with a craft knife

When using a craft knife, work on a special, self-healing cutting mat available from art suppliers. For clean cuts, the craft knife must be sharp, so keep a supply of blades handy.

1 Photocopy a template from a copyright-free book or create your own stencil design on paper. Use masking tape to secure a sheet of acetate over the design and trace the lines of the design on to the acetate, using a china marker or felt-tip pen.

2 Place the acetate on a cutting mat and cut along the lines with the craft knife, holding the knife like a pencil and turning the acetate as you cut. Stencil designs can also be transferred (see p. 96) on to stencil card and cut with a craft knife in the same way.

Wiping with a stencil brush

Using a stencil brush to wipe paint through the stencil creates lines of colour which suggest movement and energy. Remember to only use a small amount of paint, wiping any excess from the brush on to some paper towel before you begin.

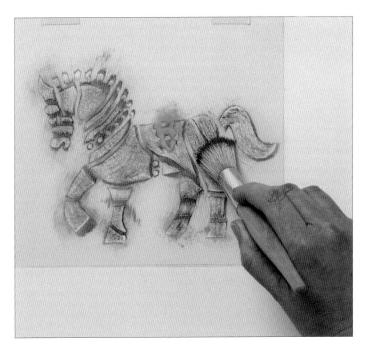

1 Secure the stencil to the surface using repositioning glue or masking tape. Pick up a small amount of paint (see p. 62) on the stencil brush and wipe the excess off on some paper towel. Wipe the paint through the stencil using the ends and sides of the bristles, following the direction of the motif's shapes.

Finished effect

The lines of paint suggest movement and create a lively stencilled effect. Here, a slightly darker colour was applied in the areas of shadow on the horse's underside and hooves to give extra definition to the design. Protect the dry decoration if desired (see pp. 122–125).

Stippling with a stencil brush

Stippling is the traditional method of stencilling with a brush and
produces an even, dotty finish. Use only a small amount of paint at a
time, wiping any excess from the brush on to a paper towel.

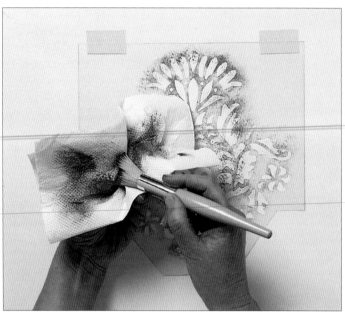

1 Secure your stencil to the surface using repositioning glue or masking
tape. Take a small amount of paint (see p. 62) on a stencil brush and wipe
the excess off on some paper towel. Dab the flat end of the stencil brush
through the stencil, holding the brush at right angles to the surface. Continue
stippling, leaving some random areas unpainted.

2 Wipe the brush on some clean paper towel to remove the first paint
colour, before picking up the second. Wipe away the excess of the
second colour on some more paper towel.

3 Use the stippling action to apply the second colour to those areas not
covered by the first colour, as well as blending the two colours in places.

Finished effect

The stippling technique produces a fine haze of tiny dots which gives the
stencil a textured finish and a neat print. Overlapping two or more colours
gives the print real depth. Protect the effect if necessary (see pp. 122–125).

Stencilling with a roller

Using a roller to stencil is a quick alternative to using brushes and gives a varied finish. However, this technique is not suitable for use with intricate stencil designs, since the roller is unable to impart paint to the smaller areas of of the motif.

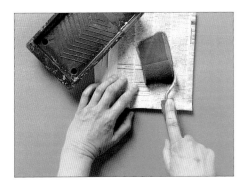

1 Load the roller with a small amount of paint (see p. 62) and test it out on some spare paper. If paint oozes out of the roller then continue rolling to remove the excess.

2 Fix the stencil to your surface using repositioning glue or masking tape. Roll the paint through the stencil in a variety of directions, leaving some random areas unpainted.

3 Roll repeatedly on spare paper to remove the first colour, before loading the second. Roll on the second colour, applying it to unpainted areas and, in some places, on top of the first colour.

Finished effect
Using a roller gives a stencil a contemporary look. In places the colour is solid whilst in other areas it has a slightly speckled appearance. Protect the effect if desired (see pp. 122–125).

Stencilling with spray paints

The myriad of fine dots produced by spray paints highlights the delicacy of a stencil design, and they are particularly suitable for use on intricate motifs, since the tiny dots of colour reach right into and define the smallest stencil cuts. Spray paints are also particularly effective on glass and fabric.

1 Fix the stencil in place using repositioning glue or masking tape. Protect the area around the stencil with newspaper. Shake the can well and test it on some spare paper. Lightly spray the first colour. A short burst will produce a small amount of spray and a delicate array of tiny dots.

2 Spray subsequent colours, using a piece of cardboard to direct the paint to a particular area, masking it from the areas you don't want covered. To produce dense patches of colour apply the spray several times: a variety of dense and light spray applications and the merging of colours gives a stencil a feeling of depth (inset). Protect if necessary when dry (see pp. 122–125).

Reverse stencilling

In this technique the usual stencil theory is reversed, and instead of applying paint through holes in the centre of the stencil, the paint is applied around the edges of the shape, producing an effect rather like a silhouette. You can use any of the paint application techniques (see pp. 85–91) when reverse stencilling, but it is best to stick to basic stencil shapes rather than intricate designs.

1 Fix the stencil in place using repositioning glue – masking tape will interfere with this technique. Apply the paint (see p. 62) around the edges of the shape using either a roller, as here, a stencil brush or spray paint. Remember to use just a small amount of paint.

Finished effect
When you remove the stencil the motif appears in the base colour and the second colour surrounds it. Protect if desired when dry (see pp. 122–125).

Stamping with found objects

A simple but impressive stamped design can be produced by dipping a household manufactured object in paint and applying it to the wall. Each motif will look different every time it is printed, which gives the design a unique, home-crafted feel.

1 You can use a variety of household objects to print on an object. Here, we have illustrated a few examples to give you inspiration. Apply a matt or mid-sheen/semi-gloss paint (see p. 62) to your found object, here a cork.

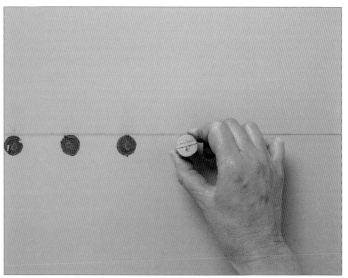

2 Test how the stamp prints on some spare paper, and adjust the amount of pressure you exert on the stamp or the amount of paint applied if necessary – too much paint will ooze out from under the stamp and ruin the intended shape. Press the cork stamp on to your surface.

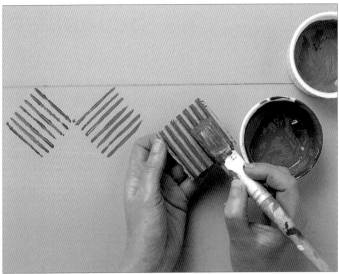

3 A nail head can be coated in paint and pressed on to the surface to produce a small, solid circle. You may find that you need to reapply paint after each stamp, or perhaps after every few stamps; this will depend on the material you are using.

4 Corrugated cardboard, usually found in packaging material, can be cut into small squares and used as stamps. In this case it is important not to press too hard as this will flatten the ridges and ruin the effect.

5 The rim of a plastic cup can be painted and stamped to make a circle or semicircle. To make a semicircle place some paper on your surface and cover it with half of the painted cup, while the other half prints on the surface.

COMBINING STAMPS

There are numerous ways in which you can combine found-object stamps to make a range of unique patterns. You could even stamp out a naive narrative scene using this technique. Here, the shape made when semicircles meet and overlap is accentuated by small white dots printed with nail heads. White cork circles sometimes overlap the semicircle pattern, and at other times sit below it, giving a changing emphasis to parts of the design.

6 The cut edge of some corrugated cardboard can also be used to stamp thin, textured lines. When you have completed your design, wait for the paints to dry before applying a coat of wax or varnish (see pp. 122–125).

Stamping with a sponge

An easy-to-use and long-lasting stamp material is the synthetic sponge.
It has a finely grained texture which works well on furniture. Wash the
sponge in water after use and leave to dry.

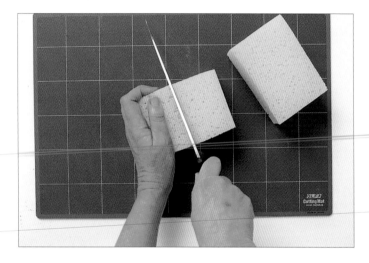

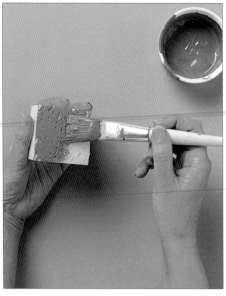

2 Use a brush or roller to apply matt or mid-sheen/semi-gloss paint (see p. 62) to the sponge.

1 Cut a sponge into the desired shape – square, rectangle, triangle – using a large sharp knife.

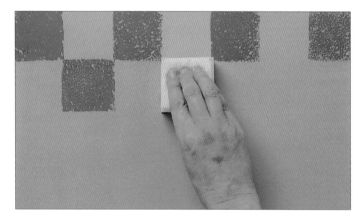

3 Press the sponge firmly against the surface to make a textured print. You will need to recoat the sponge either with every print or every two prints. Each print you make will be unique and have its own individual quality.

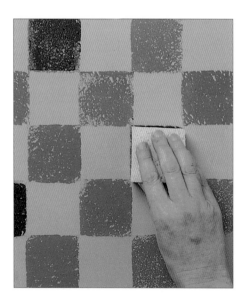

4 When the first stamped coat is dry you can overstamp in a second colour. This technique gives an interesting texture and allows some of the first colour to show through. Varnish or wax the dry finished effect if necessary (see pp. 122–125).

SPONGE SHAPES

Sponge stamps can be cut into numerous shapes and combined in a variety of ways: you are not restricted to single squares. Here, a diamond and a triangle stamp (left) combine to make a colourful border design, while rectangles and squares of different sizes (right) are joined together and overlapped to make a geometrical border.

Diamonds and triangles

Squares and rectangles

Stamping with a cut design

Large sheets of polystyrene are often used in packaging and they can be recycled to make stamps. Polystyrene is easy to cut and can be used to make quite intricate patterns. It can also be reused, but over the years the paint will cause the design to soften.

1 Use a large sharp knife to cut a block of polystyrene slightly larger than your motif.

2 You can freehand draw your design on to the polystyrene or transfer an enlarged photocopy (see p. 96). For clarity, go over light pencil lines in felt-tip pen.

3 Use a sharp craft knife to cut into the polystyrene along the lines. Then cut from the edge of the polystyrene up to the lines, cutting the excess away to leave a raised motif.

4 Apply a matt or mid-sheen/semi-gloss paint (see p. 62) to the stamp using a roller or paintbrush.

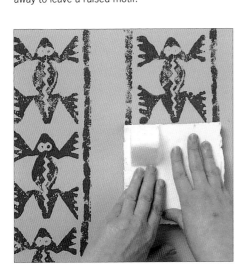

5 Press the stamp firmly on to the surface, trying to apply even pressure so that the whole motif prints successfully. Reapply paint after two or three prints.

Finished effect

Polystyrene stamps leave a wonderfully grainy and textured print. As with all stamping techniques each print is unique. Protect the dry finish with varnish or wax if necessary (see pp. 122–125).

Freehand Painting

FREEHAND PAINTING sounds quite daunting, but there are plenty of basic tricks that can help make it easier and more approachable. The first thing to remember is that painting furniture is not like painting a canvas, and never has been. Look at any old pieces of painted furniture and you will see that the hand-painting was not always straight, nor perfectly shaped. In fact the uneven paint application is part of their charm.

Using the right brushes and the correct consistency of paint is necessary to acquiring the knack. Artists' brushes are available in many shapes and sizes, so take time to choose the right one for your designs. Use artists' acrylic paints or decorator's paint (see pp. 62–63), diluted with water until free flowing: the paint should flow gently but not quickly from a brush wiped against the side of a saucer. Inks can also be used, either as they come or diluted.

Lining is used on much traditional decoration, both formal and informal. Painting a line by hand is not easy, but practice will help. Until you have had the practice however, why not paint lines with the help of masking tape?

Bright and punchy: freehand painting need not be difficult to execute.

Transferring designs

You can decorate furniture with a design found in a copyright-free book, a catalogue, on wrapping paper or a greetings card without the need for impeccable drawing skills. Simply photocopy the motif to the correct size, trace it and transfer it to the chosen surface.

1 Lay tracing paper over your chosen illustration and trace the motif using a soft pencil. Turn the tracing over and shade the outline of the image with the pencil, or use a light pigment if you are transferring to a dark surface. Turn the tracing over once more and tape it in place on your surface. Use the pencil to trace over the outline of the illustration a second time to transfer it to the surface.

2 Carefully peel back the tracing paper and check that the whole image has transferred successfully. If any areas of the outline have not come through clearly, replace the tracing paper and go over them with the pencil again. The motif can now be filled in with paint or ink.

Simple freehand motifs

You can paint simple freehand motifs using the inherent qualities of the brush shape and just a few basic hand movements. You will need to dilute the paint slightly – whether using artists' acrylics or decorators' paints (see pp. 62–63) – to make it free flowing. Test the paint on some spare paper first.

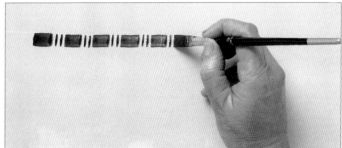

1 To paint a solid rectangle, dip a flat-ended brush in free-flowing paint and wipe off the excess on the rim of the paint container. Position the tip of your brush on the surface at a 45-degree angle and pull the brush slowly to make a rectangle. Cleanly lift the brush off and continue to repeat the motif.

2 Use the same flat-ended brush to make a thin vertical line of equal width to the rectangle. Load the brush with free-flowing paint and remove the excess. Holding the brush almost vertical to the surface, lay just the tip of the brush down, then cleanly lift it off.

3 To paint a bellflower, load a pointed brush with free-flowing paint and wipe off the excess. Position the tip of the brush on the surface to make a small dot, then pull the brush down, gradually applying more pressure to make the shape wider in the middle and applying less pressure as you reach the end until just the point of the brush touches the surface.

4 Use the same method to complete the other two petals, starting just beneath the small dot. Curve the brush out as you apply pressure, then, after reducing the pressure, finish with a small flick outwards.

5 Leaves on a stem are easily painted. Load a pointed brush with free-flowing paint and wipe off the excess on the rim of the paint container. Pull the brush down the surface, applying even pressure, to create a thin line or stem.

6 Paint leaves by working into the stem, not out from it. Start by positioning just the tip of the brush, then apply a little more pressure and drop the brush down slightly, drawing the leaf at a diagonal angle.

7 To make a looped line, load a pointed brush with free-flowing paint and wipe off the excess on the rim of the paint container. Practise the design on spare paper first until you can move your hand and the brush confidently. Hold the brush loosely in the hand and let the pressure you apply to the surface vary to apply different amounts of paint.

8 To paint curved lines like blades of grass, use a flat-ended brush. Load the brush well with free-flowing paint. Hold the brush diagonally, at about 45 degrees, and place the flat end down. Pull the brush down, lessening the angle as you go. This will make the top of the curved line pointed and the base will be wider.

9 Create simple flower motifs by painting petals and a small dot for the centre. To paint the petals, load a pointed brush with free-flowing paint. Start at the centre of the flower and pull the brush to one side just a little, to release the paint. To paint the centres, load the brush with free-flowing paint and dab the end gently on the surface. You can start with the dots or with the petals, whichever you prefer.

Three-dimensional effect

The principle of painting three-dimensional effects is based on using three tones of a single colour, the mid-tone for the main part of the object, the dark tone forms a shadow and the lightest tone indicates where light falls on the object. This simple rule can be translated to give any motif a three-dimensional look.

1 Prepare free-flowing paints (see p. 96) in three tones of one colour (inset). If the effect is to be done on a large piece of furniture the colours do not need to be very close. Draw in pencil around a coin or draw freehand circles.

2 Use a pointed artist's brush to fill the circles in with the mid-tone paint, covering the pencil lines. Leave to dry.

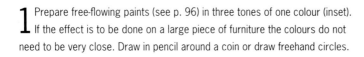

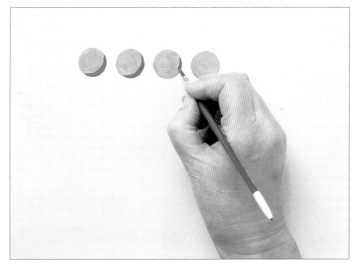

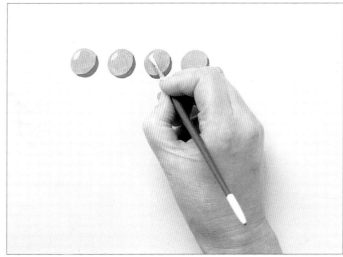

3 Towards the bottom right side of the circle, paint the darkest of the colours as if it were a shadow. Paint a shape similar to a smiling mouth, tapering out to the sides.

4 At the top left of the circle paint a small round dot in the lightest colour, to produce the effect of light catching the three-dimensional ball. Protect the dry effect with varnish or wax if necessary (see pp. 122–125).

Using masking fluid

Masking fluid is often used by watercolour artists and crafts people to mask areas they don't want painted. Available from art suppliers, masking fluid protects the surface from anything that is put on top of it. It dries to a rubbery consistency that can be peeled off. You must wash your brush immediately after using masking fluid, before the medium dries.

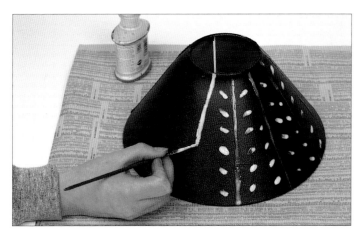

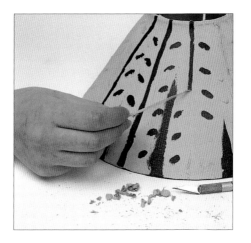

1 Use an artist's brush to paint on the masking fluid quite generously. Here we are using a simple freehand motif but you could transfer a design (see p. 96) and fill it in with masking fluid. As the fluid dries it turns dark yellow.

2 When the fluid has completely dried, paint over it with a matt or mid-sheen/semi-gloss paint (see p. 62). Here, we have left some areas unpainted.

3 When the paint has dried, peel off the rubbery masking fluid. You may need to use a craft knife to lift some areas of fluid, but take care not to scratch the paintwork. Protect the dry finished effect with varnish or wax (see pp. 122–125).

Lining with masking tape

Low-tack masking tape can be a great tool when painting straight
lines. Use it to protect the surface on either side of the line. You can
also use this technique to paint wide stripes.

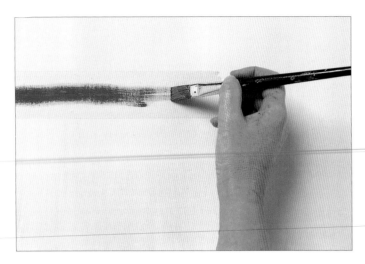

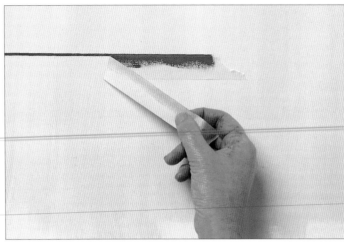

1 Position two parallel strips of masking tape, leaving a gap to the width of
your choice. Load a small amount of paint (see p. 62) on a stiff bristle
brush and paint over the gap, overlapping on to the masking tape.

2 When you have built up a solid layer of paint, peel away the masking tape
as soon as possible, to prevent it from adhering too strongly to the
surface beneath.

Freehand lining

A thin line just inside the edge of a piece of furniture emphasizes the shape of the
object beautifully, but the painting technique demands a degree of hand control.
You will need to dilute the paint slightly – whether it be artists' acrylics or
decorators' paints (see pp. 62–63) – until it is free flowing. Test the consistency of
the paint on some spare paper first.

2 Load the brush well with paint:
you need to be able to complete
one whole line in a single attempt.
Guide the brush along the surface
resting your little finger against the
edge of the surface to guide your
hand. Try not to watch the brush but
keep your eye on the area just in
front of it, and apply even pressure
throughout, otherwise your line will
vary in thickness. If you do run out of
paint in the middle of a line, restart
before the break, going back over
some of the already painted line to
pick up the flow.

1 First draw some guidelines with a pencil or
coloured pencil – use a light colour on a dark
surface and a dark colour on a light surface. You
can use a ruler at this stage.

3 To indicate a shadow, add a thin dark line on the inside of the main line. Do this only when the first line is dry, that way if you make a mistake it can be easily wiped off with a damp cloth.

4 When the previous paints are completely dry, apply a thin, lighter line to the outside edge of the main line to act as a highlight and complete this classic effect.

5 To paint a further line, slightly inset from the original, first mark a guideline in pencil. Here, the line is still fairly close to the edge and the hand can rest on it for guidance, whilst holding the pencil at an angle close to the surface. Alternatively you can use a ruler.

6 Place a straight piece of wood at a comfortable distance from the line to rest your guiding finger on. When the effect is dry, protect with varnish or wax if desired (see pp. 122–125).

CLASSIC CORNERS

Corner designs really emphasize an object's shape and are an elaborate addition to any freehand lining. Using the same principles of freehand lining, the decorative painter can practise the technique and produce unique corner motifs.

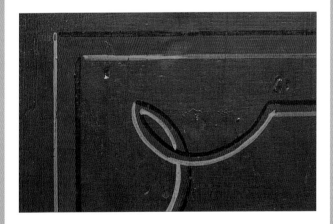

Basic penwork

Decorating with ink is a traditional technique which produces a solid, opaque block of decoration. India ink – which is black – and sepia – a brown ink – are commonly used. Waterproof drawing inks and mapping pens to apply the ink are available from art suppliers, or you can use ordinary writing ink which is more transparent and is not waterproof. If you are using ink on wood it is a good idea to seal the surface first (see p. 71).

1 Transfer a design (see p. 96) on to the surface. Dip the nib of a mapping pen in some ink and remove the excess ink on a piece of spare paper. First draw around an individual shape, then fill it in with ink.

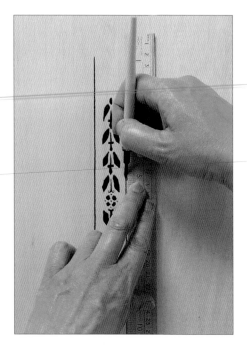

2 Using a ruler to draw straight lines with ink is a technique that should be practised before being applied to the surface. Load the nib with ink, raise the ruler slightly, then draw a line straight up until the ink runs out. To restart a line start by overlapping a small section of the previous line. Protect if necessary when dry (see pp. 122–125).

Filling in the background

Instead of filling in the design with ink, another traditional penwork technique is to fill in the background. For this you will need a fine artist's brush as well as a mapping pen to apply the ink. When using ink on wood it is a good idea to seal the surface first (see p. 71).

Transfer a design (see p. 96) on to the surface. Dip the nib of a mapping pen in some ink and remove the excess on spare paper. Draw the outline of the design using the pen. Dip a fine artist's brush in ink, remove excess on a sheet of spare paper and use it to carefully fill in the area around the outside of the design. When the first coat is dry apply a second layer of ink for a more solid effect. Protect the dry finished effect if necessary (see pp. 122–125).

Using diluted ink

By diluting ink you will achieve a softer finish than the solid, opaque look of traditional penwork. Instead, a translucent effect is achieved, with some of the background showing through the ink. Combine this with undiluted ink for details, depth and shadows. If you are using ink on wood it is a good idea to seal the surface first (see p. 71).

1 Transfer a design (see p. 96) on to the surface and fill in the outline with undiluted ink, using a mapping pen (see *Basic penwork*, p. 102). Dilute the ink, beginning with a ratio of one part ink to one part water. Test the ink on some spare paper or an unseen surface and adjust the ratio if desired. Use a fine artist's brush to apply the diluted ink to areas of the design, such as the central parts of the leaves in this motif.

2 To give definition to the design you can freehand paint small details in undiluted ink using a mapping pen. Here we have added veins to the leaves. Protect with varnish or wax when dry, if necessary (see pp. 122–125).

USING A CALLIGRAPHY PEN

Instead of using a mapping pen, a variety of simple shapes and patterns can be drawn in ink using a calligraphy pen with different nibs. Here, an angled, square-ended nib has been used, and just a few simple penstrokes creates an impressive range of motifs.

Simple diamonds

Thin line on the upward strokes and thick line on the downward strokes

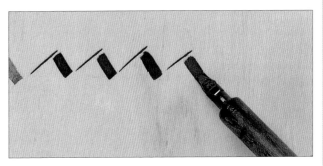

Thin line on the upward and downward strokes and thick line on the horizontal strokes

Looped line widens and narrows

Gilding

ETALLIC EFFECTS, whether gold, copper or silver, give a piece of furniture brightness and light and can be achieved using either metal leaf or bronze powders. The idea of gilding using metal leaf sounds to many people a very difficult undertaking. In fact, this is not the case, especially since the advent of modern, easy-to-use materials such as imitation metal leaf and water-based gold size. If you are unsure, however, you might want to begin with the distressing technique. Here the metal leaf is applied deliberately imperfectly since gaps, tears and folds will help reveal the contrasting colour underneath when wax and steel wool are applied.

Bronze powders give a solid but soft metallic effect and are also easy to use. They can be used on their own or mixed with either wax or varnish. All metallic effects look most effective over a matt-painted background (see p. 62) and they must be protected with varnish (see pp. 122–123) to prevent tarnishing.

Gilding does not have to be applied to traditional pieces of furniture like ornate carved frames and side tables. It can be used boldly and loosely using the rectangular edges of the leaf in an abstract way and mixing aluminium, copper and Dutch metal.

Using metal leaf

Here we have used Dutch metal leaf which imitates gold, but aluminium, which imitates silver, and copper are also readily available and should be applied in the same way. Water-based gold size is white when applied, but turns transparent and shiny as it dries. Do not attempt to apply the metal leaf until the size has become clear. Metal leaf must be handled with care, so allow yourself plenty of time to work: the size remains tacky indefinitely so you do not need to worry about working quickly.

1 Apply the size to the surface using a brush. Leave it to dry for a few minutes. As the white size dries it becomes transparent, but its shine means it remains visible.

2 Dust your hands with French chalk or talcum powder to help prevent the metal leaf sticking to your fingers.

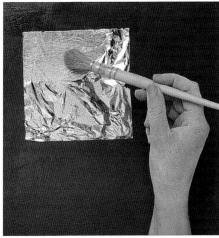

4 Use a gilder's mop or soft brush to smooth the leaf into place, using a gentle dabbing action rather than wiping it.

3 Lift the metal leaf and gently manoeuvre your hands until you are holding it comfortably. Aim to position one edge of the leaf on the size and gradually ease the rest of the sheet into place. If a sheet tears try to match up the edges as closely as possible.

5 Continue applying metal leaf to the surface, slightly overlapping the sheets each time. Using the gilder's mop or soft brush gently wipe away the excess metal leaf, saving the excess for the next stage.

6 When the excess leaf is wiped away it will probably reveal a few gaps that have not been covered with metal leaf. These can easily be filled with the excess leaf you have collected. Pick up a piece of excess leaf using the tip of your finger or the gilder's mop. Press the piece into the gap. If at first it does not adhere, apply a little more size to the exposed surface and try again.

7 When all the gaps are filled use the gilder's mop or soft brush to gently wipe away the last remaining excess leaf. The metal leaf finish must be varnished (see pp. 122–123) to protect it and prevent it tarnishing.

TRANSFER METAL LEAF

An alternative to the traditional 'loose' metal leaf, is a material called 'transfer' metal leaf. It has a waxed-paper backing which makes it easy to handle, but is not as readily available as loose leaf.

Size the surface as in Step 1 of *Using metal leaf* (see p. 104). Hold the transfer metal leaf by the overhanging edges of the waxed-paper backing and position it on the size. Smooth the waxed paper with your fingers, until it becomes loose and can be easily peeled away. Continue by following Steps 5–7.

Distressing metal leaf

Metal leaf will naturally wear away over the years, especially around those areas of an object that get the most use. This effect can be re-created by distressing a newly applied layer of metal leaf with wax and steel wool. The technique can also be adapted for a contemporary look by using brightly coloured base coats or distressing the leaf in particular shapes.

1 Cover the surface with metal leaf (see pp. 104–105), but don't worry if the leaf creases or tears. Dip some very fine steel wool in clear, neutral or coloured wax and rub it over the gilded surface.

2 Take a clean piece of steel wool and use it to rub over parts of the gilded surface to remove some of the metal leaf.

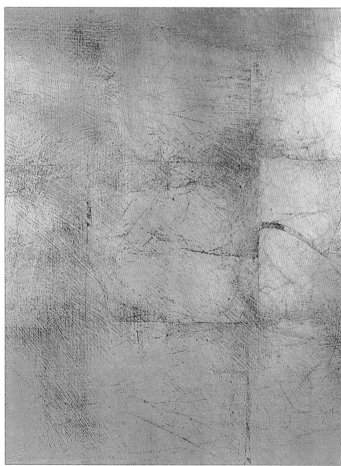

3 When you have finished distressing, leave the wax to harden following your product's instructions. The wax will have dulled the metal leaf but it can now be buffed to a mellow shine using a soft, clean cotton cloth.

Finished effect

Where the metal leaf has been distressed, the colour beneath can be seen as if the surface has naturally aged through wear and tear. You can use this technique to disguise or remove any faults made while applying metal leaf.

Incising through paint

Metal leaf revealed through a design in paint looks wonderful, especially if the paint is very matt and in stark contrast to the shiny leaf. You can use all kinds of materials to incise through the wet paint, but make sure that the incising tool is firm enough to remove the paint and be controlled, and yet soft enough not to break the metal leaf.

1 Protect a layer of metal leaf (see pp. 104–105) with a coat of varnish (see pp. 122–123). When dry, cover the protected leaf with a coat of matt paint (see p. 62).

2 While the paint is still wet, use firm materials which have soft edges to remove the paint and reveal the metal leaf beneath. Cotton buds work well because they absorb the paint quickly, but you will need plenty on hand.

3 A small plastic comb used for paint effects (see p. 79), or a similar implement made out of cardboard, produces a series of lines.

4 Blu-Tack ®/mounting putty absorbs the paint and can be used to make small dots. Reform if often as it becomes saturated with paint.

5 Use a very thin piece of cork to produce a clean thin line. Regularly wipe excess paint from the cork with a cloth.

6 The edge of a piece of cardboard will produce a textured mark because it does not remove the paint cleanly.

7 A cork cut in half also creates a textured, soft mark which randomly removes the paint. When you have completed your design, allow the paint to dry before protecting with varnish (see pp. 122–123).

Using bronze powders

Bronze powders are very fine metallic powders that come in a wide range of colours. When brushed on to a design painted in gold size they form a solid metallic covering. Because they are so fine, bronze powders should be handled in a draught-free environment and it is advisable to wear a face mask.

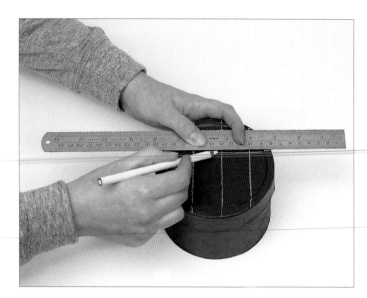

1 First mark out your design. Here, we have used a simple geometric pattern but you could transfer a design (see p. 96) or draw through a stencil.

2 Use a brush to apply water-based gold size to the design. Leave the size for a few minutes until it is transparent rather than white.

4 Use different-coloured bronze powders to add depth to the design. Here, we have used a copper powder to complement the gold.

3 Sprinkle some bronze powder on to your surface just next to the tacky size. Then use a soft brush to gently push the powder on to the size. Make sure the brush is dry or the powders will smudge. The bronze powder will adhere to the size and excess powder can be simply brushed away.

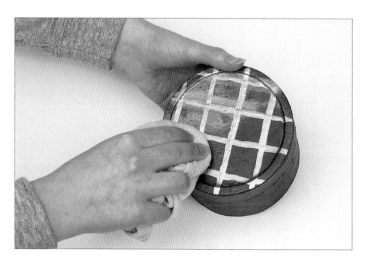

5 When you have covered all the size use a soft, dry cloth to wipe away the excess powder, revealing the design. Varnish (see pp. 122–123) the effect to prevent it from tarnishing.

Metallic paint

Metallic paints are easy and quick to use, but they will never be as bright as metal leaf or bronze powders used on their own. You can buy commercial brands of metallic paint or you can make your own by mixing bronze powders with varnish (see p. 66): a water-based varnish is best since it can be diluted with water and is inexpensive to buy. Do not mix too much varnish and bronze powder at one time because the paint does not keep well.

1 Start by pouring a little varnish into a small bowl. Use a teaspoon or palette knife to carefully add small quantities of bronze powder to the varnish.

2 Use a brush to mix the powder and varnish together until completely blended. Aim to create an opaque paint that is still runny, and experiment with the ratio of bronze powder to varnish until you reach the ideal consistency.

3 To completely cover a surface, use the metallic paint in the same way as an ordinary paint (see p. 72). However, if you miss an area, you must wait until the first coat is completely dry before retouching.

4 To paint small designs, dilute the metallic paint with a little water until it is free flowing, and apply it with a fine artist's brush. You will need to clean your brush frequently to prevent it becoming clogged with dried paint.

Metallic wax

Traditionally metallic waxes were used on the tips of carved objects, to give a hint of gold. A metallic wax is not as bright as metal leaf or bronze powder, but it produces a beautiful mellow, soft tone. It is also easy to make, using clear or neutral wax and bronze powder, and quick to use. Metallic wax keeps well in an airtight container so feel free to make as much as you like at one time.

1 Put equal quantities of clear or neutral wax and bronze powder in a small container and mix them together with a palette knife. When the two materials are completely blended, dip the tip of your finger into the wax to pick some up.

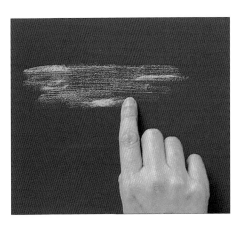

2 Using your finger, wipe the wax smoothly on to the surface in one direction. The wax looks equally good whether applied solidly, or lightly with the colour beneath showing through.

Decoupage

SIMPLY CUTTING OUT paper pictures and gluing them to a surface opens up a great variety of decorating opportunities. The technique can be used to mimic the traditional Victorian style of overlapping cutouts, to imitate hand painting or to produce modern, abstract designs. The choice of papers you can use for decoupage is as versatile as the technique, from a wide range of exciting wrapping papers – patterned, plain, printed with stone or wood effects or tissue paper – original prints, high quality magazines, specialist copyright-free books and traditional Victorian scraps, the sky really is the limit.

The basic technique

There is a wealth of paper sources which can be used for decoupage, including catalogues, postcards and wrapping paper. Copyright laws vary from country to country, but as a rule you must not photocopy or sell an image that is under copyright to someone else, but should write to the copyright holder asking for their permission. Most copyright holders will be happy to give permission but they will charge you if your design is for commercial use.

1 Use good quality, sharp scissors to cut out your motif. Here, designs are taken from wrapping paper. Remember that you can cut out the motif to your own specifications, for example the fishing lines on the back of this boat are too thin to cut out, so, instead, you can cut them off.

2 Apply the glue to your surface. You can use any thin paper glue, starch glue or white craft glue. To mark the shape of your motif on the surface before applying the glue, position the motif and wipe over its edges with a damp sponge. The water darkens the edges around the shape, leaving a clear boundary for you to apply the glue within.

3 Carefully place the motif over the glue, starting with one section of the paper shape and smoothing the rest into position. A damp sponge will help you to position the motif and the moisture will allow the paper to stretch and move.

4 Gently wipe the motif with a damp sponge, working from the centre to the edges, to remove air bubbles and trapped glue. Use the sponge to remove excess glue from the area surrounding the motif.

5 Continue applying motifs over your object. If your piece has drawers or doors it can look great to position the motifs so that they overlap the joints and continue around corners. Simply cut through the motif with a craft knife at the point where it overlaps a door or drawer joint.

6 Apply a varnish of your choice (see pp. 122–123) using a good quality varnish brush. Paint the varnish on with the brush at an angle close to the surface, and bring the brush to an angle of almost 90 degrees to the surface to feather the varnish out. Let the varnish dry thoroughly before applying another coat. The traditional aim of varnishing decoupage was to disguise the ridge between the paper and the surface and so, often, upward of ten coats were required. You do not need to apply this many coats, but a minimum of three coats is advisable.

COMPOSITIONAL DECOUPAGE

By selecting a number of images that are roughly in proportion to each other, you can use decoupage to create a narrative scene, almost like a painting. On this chest of drawers a feeling of depth is achieved with the use of perspective. The cutout of the cows is slightly larger than the cutout of the horses and their cart, which makes it look like the cows are at the front of the scene and the cart is a short distance behind them. The background has been lightly painted with different colours to give the impression of land and sky, while simple freehand motifs (see pp. 97–98) like grass and shadows have also been added.

The print room technique

The traditional print room technique was an 18th-century method of imitating an arrangement of framed paintings on a wall using prints adorned with paper frames, garlands, ribbons and swags. The technique can be adapted for furniture by using a single print and giving it a paper frame adapted from a paper border. You can buy borders and accessories produced specifically for print room work from specialist paper shops, or by mail order.

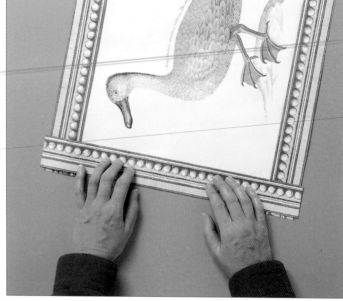

1 To measure and cut your frame, first draw a thin pencil line on your print, marking where you want the inside of the frame to align. Position small tabs of masking tape on the underside of the print, sticky side up.

2 Cut your border into four lengths to surround the print, making sure that the lengths overlap each corner. Align the border lengths with the pencil line and secure them to the masking tape.

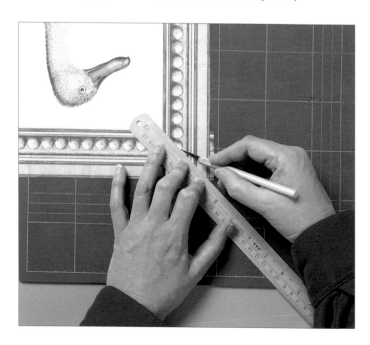

4 When you remove the sections of cut border, you will be left with a perfect corner join.

3 Place the print and borders on a cutting mat and position a metal ruler from corner to corner of an overlapping border. Use a sharp craft knife to cut along the ruler, cutting through the two overlapping borders. Don't worry if you also cut through the print.

6 Place the print upside down on some spare paper and use a flat-ended paintbrush to apply a generous amount of glue. A starch glue is particularly good for this technique.

5 Remove the borders and masking tape tabs from the print before immersing it in water for a few minutes. Use a large container that will allow the print to remain flat while it is immersed.

7 Carefully position the prepared print on the surface. Dab it with a damp sponge to help it adhere and remove any air bubbles.

COLOURING PRINTS

It is often necessary to colour a black and white print, as they can appear very stark against a coloured background. If you want a new print to look like an old print then soaking it in tea or sprinkling a very small amount of instant coffee on a dampened print gives a good yellowed-with-age look. Alternatively, use a sponge to wipe the print with very dilute paint to achieve a pale colour (below). Watercolour pencils can be used to fill in more than one colour.

8 Glue the borders in position in the same way, remembering to align them with the pencil marks on the print. Here, we have also glued on a pair of swags stemming from the base of the print. When using real prints it is best not to varnish the finished effect, you may want to remove the prints at a later stage.

Making your own designs

Making your own decoupage motifs is very rewarding. A ready-cut stencil makes a great template for a unique decoupage motif which can be cut from abstract paper and repeated many times without ever looking the same. An exactly symmetrical motif can be cut by drawing half a design on to paper, folding the paper in half along the edges of the half-motif and cutting along the motif lines. This type of design is equally effective whether cut from plain or patterned paper.

Using a stencil template

1 Cut your chosen paper so that it is the same size as the stencil. This will make the paper much easier to handle.

2 Place the stencil over the underside of the paper and draw through it with a pencil.

3 Carefully cut out all the elements of the motif.

4 Place the main element of the motif in position on the surface. Carefully re-lay the stencil over the main element and draw through the stencil on to the surface. Apply glue to the surface inside the pencil marks.

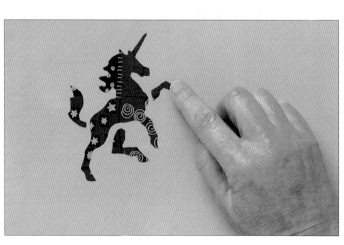

5 Press the paper pieces into position on the glue and follow Steps 4–6 of *The basic technique* (see p. 111) to finish.

Symmetrical designs

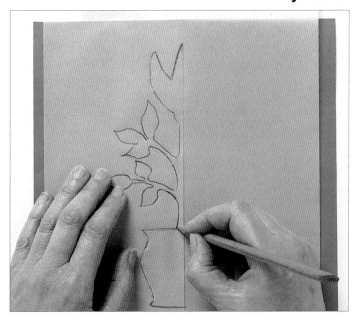

1 Draw a line down the centre of a simple symmetrical motif and trace half of the design. Fold some coloured paper in half and transfer (see p. 96) the half-motif on to the paper, aligning it with the centre fold.

2 Refold the coloured paper along the existing fold line. Cut out the half-motif following the pencil marks.

3 Unfold the cut-out motif to reveal a perfectly symmetrical design. Fix the motif to your surface following Steps 2–6 of *The basic technique* (see pp. 110–111).

GEOMETRIC DESIGNS

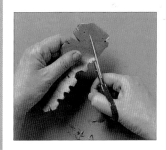

To create a geometric paper motif with a handmade look, fold a sheet in half several times and cut notches of various widths and shapes into the folded edges. Then follow Steps 2–6 of *The basic technique* (see pp. 110–111) to fix the motif.

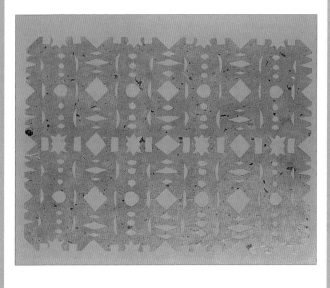

Faux marquetry

Some wonderful effects, reminiscent of traditional marquetry, can be created using decoupage techniques. Wood- and stone-effect papers are available from good paper shops and can be used against a wood or stone background to imitate inlaid effects on pieces of furniture.

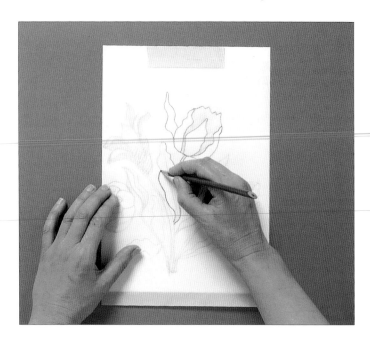

1 Choose a design with simple shapes that can be adapted for use with three wood-effect papers. Trace the design.

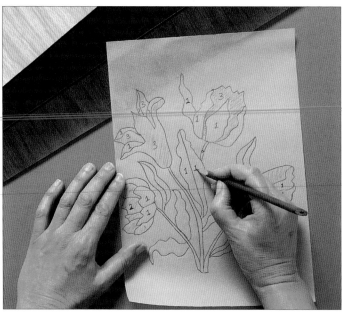

2 Assign a number to each shape in the design that corresponds to a wood-effect paper – here for example, 1 is a light paper, 2 is a red paper and 3 is a dark paper.

3 Over some spare paper, turn the tracing paper over and shade over the traced lines with a pencil.

4 Turn the tracing paper over again and position it on the first wood-effect paper. Retrace the outlines of the shapes that correspond to that paper, transferring the designs. Do the same for the other shapes and wood-effect papers. If you have some intricate shapes, such as the flower-heads here, aim to cut one large shape first – the whole flower-head – and then cut the smaller shapes – the petals – which can be glued over the top.

5 Cut out all the shapes, either using a sharp craft knife over a cutting mat or with a pair of sharp, good quality scissors.

6 Transfer the whole design on to the surface to be decorated, pressing firmly to make sure all the pencil lines show through.

7 Glue the shapes in position following Step 3 of *The basic technique* (see p. 110) and using the numbered tracing as a guide. Wipe away excess glue and expel any air bubbles with a damp sponge.

8 Try to add touches of extra dimension by overlapping papers with the woodgrains running in different directions. Glue smaller elements on top of the large elements.

Finished effect

The finished effect imitates the look of a design inlaid in wood, similar to traditional marquetry techniques. A similar effect can be achieved by using stone-effect papers on a stone background. Varnish the effect (see Step 6 of *The basic technique*, p. 111).

Ageing Techniques

THE EFFECTS OF TIME and natural wear and tear are revealed on painted furniture in two ways, peeling paint or an aged patina – a natural film that forms with age and usually has a glossy sheen or veiled cloudiness. These effects can be recreated on new or newly decorated pieces of furniture using waxes, varnishes and the specialist mediums crackleglaze and crackle varnish. They are all techniques that can be used alone or be applied over previous decoration such as stencilling, freehand painting or decoupage. Remember that once a piece has been waxed, varnish cannot be applied.

Distressing with wax

Wax – whether clear or dark – softens water-based paint, making it easier to distress with steel wool and reveal the colour beneath, giving a look of natural wear and tear. Use matt paints which will allow the wax to be absorbed into the surface, rather than a sheen paint which will reject the wax.

1 Paint your object with a solid coat of matt paint (see p. 62) and leave to dry for a few hours.

2 Apply a second coat of matt paint in random areas, keeping it fairly thin throughout. Leave to dry.

3 Dip some fine steel wool in furniture wax and rub it into the surface. You can use clear or dark wax (see p. 124).

4 As the wax is absorbed, rub the surface with fine steel wool to remove some paint. Vary the pressure you use to reveal the base colour in some places and the original surface in others.

5 Apply another layer of wax to the distressed surface to protect the effect and use a soft cloth to buff it to a sheen.

Distressing varnish

Distressing varnish with steel wool and paint gives your furniture an aged look, as if wear and tear and dirt have taken their toll on an antique treasure. Remember that the varnish must be completely dry before you scratch it, otherwise the whole coat will just peel away.

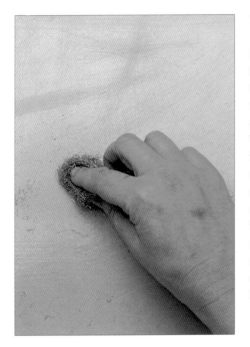

1 Apply two to three coats of water-based varnish (see pp. 122–123) making sure each coat is completely dry before applying the next. When the final coat is thoroughly dry, scratch into the surface using coarse steel wool. Do not rub the surface in a circular motion, but use straight lines in all directions and of all lengths.

2 Pick up some dark-coloured matt paint (see p. 62) on a bristle brush and rub it into the scratchmarks. Use as many different colours as you like.

3 Before the paint is dry, rub firmly over the surface with a cotton cloth to push the paint right into the scratchmarks and remove the excess paint.

4 Wipe off the final traces of excess paint using a damp sponge – the paint should only be visible in the scratchmarks. When the paint is dry, apply a final coat of varnish to protect the effect.

Crackle varnish

To imitate the network of fine cracks often seen in the varnish of antique paintings and pieces of furniture, a commercial two-part medium can be used. This consists of two varnishes which react with each other to produce the cracks. Artists' oil paints are then used to emphasize the cracks. This technique will not work on a surface that is too absorbent, so apply a few coats of matt paint (see p. 62) or varnish (see pp. 122–123) to seal such a surface.

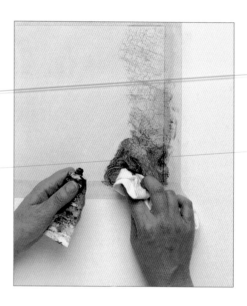

1 Apply an even coat of the first varnish to a clean surface that is smooth and not too absorbent. A thick coat at this stage will mean thicker cracks and the whole effect will take longer to dry.

2 When the first varnish coat is partly dry and still a little tacky, apply a thin coat of the second varnish. As the surface dries, cracks will begin to appear. You can speed up the drying process with a hair-drier set to a low heat – if it is too hot the top layer will simply peel off.

3 When the surface is completely dry, rub some dark-coloured artist's oil paint into the cracks using a cotton cloth. While the paint is still wet, use a clean cotton cloth to wipe away the excess, leaving paint in the cracks only.

Finished effect
The fine cracks running all over the surface are emphasized by the colour added to them, as if they have filled with dirt over the years.

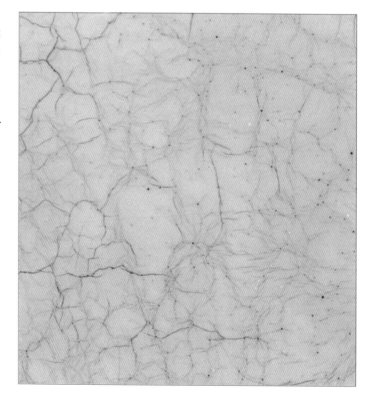

4 Protect the surface, when dry, with a coat of oil-based varnish (see pp. 122–123) or the medium recommended by your product.

Crackleglaze

To imitate the look of paint that has cracked or peeled away from the surface over the years, use a commercial crackleglaze medium applied between two coats of water-based paint. This technique will not work on an absorbent surface, so prepare such a surface with a few coats of matt paint (see p. 62) or varnish (see pp. 122–123). Take great care not to overbrush the final coat of paint and protect the finished effect with oil-based varnish – water-based varnish will crack – to stop the paint flaking off.

1 Apply an even coat of matt paint (see p. 62) to the surface. Leave to dry for a few hours.

2 Use a clean brush to apply an even coat of crackleglaze medium to the surface. A thick coat of crackleglaze will result in large cracks and a thin coat will produce small cracks. Leave to dry.

3 When the crackleglaze is completely dry, apply another coat of matt paint in a contrasting colour. Do not overbrush and apply the paint in all directions. As the paint dries, the crackleglaze beneath causes it to crack, revealing the base colour and imitating peeling paint. When the paint is dry, protect the effect with a coat of oil-based varnish (see pp. 122–123) or the medium recommended by your product.

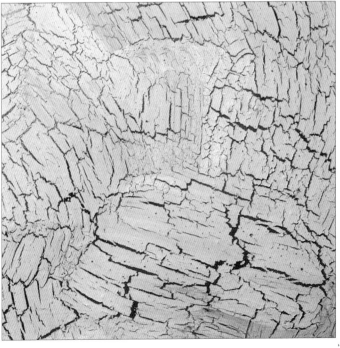

Finished effect

When you use contrasting colours, the cracks stand out very clearly. The peeling paint effect could also be produced with similar paint colours for a more subtle effect.

Varnish and Wax

ONCE YOU HAVE decorated your furniture and created a piece to be proud of, you will naturally want to protect it from scuffs, chips, heat and water. Varnishes and waxes can change the look of your work, so take time to look at the qualities of the different varnishes and waxes (see *Types of varnish*, below, and *Types of wax*, p. 124) before committing.

Varnish provides strong protection and is almost invisible. Varnish should not distract the eye from the original decoration, so it is important to apply it carefully to avoid lumps and bumps.

Varnish is stronger than wax, but that is not to say that wax is not a good protection. Although not effective against heavy spillages of water, wax will protect furniture well. It can be renewed easily and frequently and, unlike varnish, wax will not chip away, taking the paint with it. If, when you apply a dark or coloured wax, you are unhappy with the result, use a clear wax to wipe it away. If the wax has dried you will need to use a commercial furniture cleaner to remove it (see p. 68).

Multiple coats of gloss varnish make an attractive finish.

Types of varnish

On this blue-painted background four types of varnish have been used to illustrate the different finish each one imparts. Water-based varnishes are also known as acrylic varnishes, while oil-based varnishes are often called polyurethane varnishes.

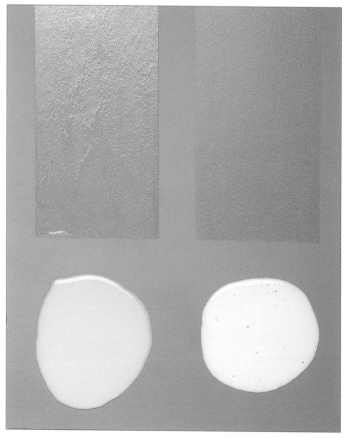

Gloss water-based varnish   Flat water-based varnish   Coloured water-based varnish   Oil-based varnish

Applying varnish

Apply water- and oil-based varnishes in the same way, aiming for thin
and even layers. Try to work in a dust-free environment so that specks
don't settle on the surface while the varnish is still wet.

1 Make sure your surface is free of dust and
grease and is smooth and dry. Load a flat-
ended varnish brush with varnish and, keeping
the brush at a low angle to the surface, apply a
layer of varnish.

2 When the brush is empty of varnish alter the
position of your hand so that the brush is at a
90-degree angle to the surface, and feather the
varnish with the tip of the brush until it is spread
as thinly as possible. Leave to dry and apply a
second coat if necessary.

3 If the surface reveals any blemishes, or
specks of dust have settled on the varnish,
wrap some wet-and-dry sandpaper around a
wooden block and dip it in water. Rub gently over
the surface to remedy the blemishes.

Colouring varnish

You can colour a water- or oil-based varnish using the pigment of your
choice, aiming for a mixture that, although coloured, remains
transparent. Remember that if you are varnishing an object that is
already coloured the base colour is likely to affect the varnish colour.

1 Put some coloured pigment in a bowl (about 3 level teaspoons of pigment
to 1 pint/600ml of varnish) and press out any lumps. Add the varnish a
little at a time, stirring continuously with the brush. Aim to produce a mixture
that is coloured but still transparent.

2 Apply the varnish using a varnish brush and feathering it out thinly
(see Applying varnish, above).

Types of wax

On this blue-green background, four types of wax have been used to
illustrate the different finish each one imparts.

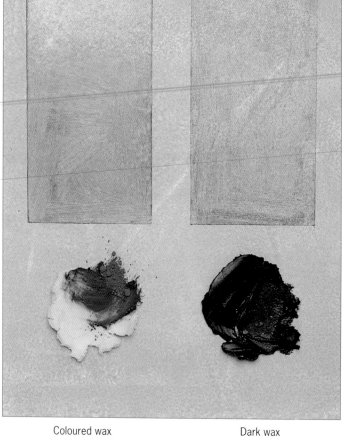

Clear wax   Neutral wax   Coloured wax   Dark wax

Applying wax

Wax protects only when the solvents inherent in the material are
absorbed into the surface. Therefore, wax should be used only on
absorbent surfaces: shiny surfaces such as metal, plastic or gloss paints
and varnishes will reject the wax.

1 Pick up some wax
on fine-grade steel
wool and rub it gently
into the surface. Allow
the wax solvents to
sink into the surface
until it is no longer wet
to the touch.

2 When the surface
is no longer tacky
it can be polished to a
soft sheen with a
polishing brush, as
here, or a soft, clean
cotton cloth.

Liming

This traditional technique uses white wax to emphasize the grain in a
wooden surface. You can buy white wax as a commercial product or mix
white pigment with clear or neutral wax (see *Colouring wax*, below).

1 Although not essential, it can be useful to open up the grain of the wood before liming by rubbing it hard with a phosphor bronze wire brush, following the grain.

2 Take some white wax on fine-grade steel wool and rub it generously across the surface. First work across the grain and then along it. Allow the solvents to absorb into the wood, but do not let the wax dry out completely.

3 Take a fresh piece of fine-grade steel wool and rub over the surface again, in both directions, removing excess wax.

4 Take some clear wax on a fresh piece of steel wool and rub this over the surface, pushing the white wax right into the woodgrain.

Colouring wax

You can make many different-coloured waxes by mixing the pigment
of your choice with clear or neutral wax. Remember that if you are
waxing an object that is already coloured, the base colour is likely to
affect the wax colour.

5 When the solvents of the clear wax have been absorbed and the surface is no longer tacky, use a clean, soft cotton cloth to polish the finish to a subtle sheen.

Take some clear or neutral wax in a container and add coloured pigment to it little by little. Use a palette knife to mix the wax and pigment until you reach the desired intensity of colour. Apply the wax as normal (see *Applying wax*, p. 124).

Index

SUPPLIERS

Below is a list of suppliers of Annie Sloan's paints in the UK, listed alphabetically by county, and similar paint and equipment stockists in the US and Canada, ordered by state. Annie Sloan products are available mail order by calling the Annie Sloan order line on 0870 6010082 (44 870 6010082 from outside the UK). Details of products can be found on Annie's internet site at www.anniesloan.com and Annie can also be contacted by e-mail at paint@anniesloan.com

ENGLAND

Fanny's Antique Centre
1 Lynmouth Road, Reading
Berks RG1 8DD
Tel: 01189 508261 & 01189 691979

The Natural Fabric Co.
Wessex Place, 127 High Street
Hungerford, Berks RG17 0DL
Tel: 01488 684002

Marlow Antiques Centre
35 Station Road, Marlow
Bucks SL7 1NN
Tel: 01628 473223

Wrights of Lymm Ltd
Millers Lane, Lymm
Cheshire WA13 9RG
Tel: 01925 752226

Serendipity
12 Devonshire Street, Penrith
Cumbria CA11 7SR
Tel: 01768 895 977

The Stencil Shop
Eyam Hall Craft Centre, Eyam
Hope Valley, Derbys S32 5QW
Tel: 01433 639001

Bailey Paints
Griffin Mill Estate, London Road
New Stroud,Thrupp, Glos GL5 2AZ
Tel: 01453 882237

Burwoods
14 The Square, Winchester
Hants SO23 9ES
Tel: 01962 854716

Webbs of Tenterden
51 High Street, Tenterden
Kent TN30 6BH
Tel: 01580 762132

Period Effects
4 Church Street, Lutterworth
Leics LE17 4AW
Tel: 01455 553049

John Jones
4 Morris Place, Off Stroud Green Road
Finsbury Park, London N4 3JG
Tel: 0171 281 5439

Interiors of Chiswick
454–458 Chiswick High Road
London W4 5TT
Tel: 0181 994 0073

London Graphic Centre
16–18 Shelton Street, Covent Garden
London WC2 9JJ
Tel: 0171 240 0095

Paint & Paper Ltd
11 Hellesdon Park Ind. Est.
Drayton Road, Norwich
Norfolk NR6 5DR
Tel: 01603 400777

Relics of Witney
35 Bridge Street, Witney
Oxon OX8 6DA
Tel: 01993 704611

Half a Sixpence
The Borough Mall, Wedmore
Somerset BS28 4EB
Tel: 01934 713331

Welcome Home Gift Shop
18a Warwick Street, Worthing
Sussex BN11 3DJ
Tel: 01903 215542

Trend of Worcester
14 Friar Street, Worcester WR1 2RZ
Tel: 01905 28178

NORTHERN IRELAND
Paint Magic
59 High Street, Holywood
Co. Down BT18 9AQ
Tel: 01232 421881

SCOTLAND

Shapes
Wester Inches Farm House
Inverness IV2 5BG
Tel: 01463 230378

USA AND CANADA

Contact any of the following businesses to find the store location nearest to you. Craft and paint supplies.

Delta Technical Coatings
2550 Pellissier Place, Whittier
CA 90601
Tel: (800) 423-4135

CraftCo Industries, Inc.
410 Wentworth Street North, Hamilton
Ontario, Canada, L8L 5WS
Tel: (800) 661-0010
Web site: http://www.craftco.com

Back Street, Inc.
3905 Steve Reynolds Blvd.
Norcross, GA 30093
Tel: (770) 381-7373
Fax: (770) 381-6424

Home Depot U.S.A., Inc.
2455 Paces Ferry Road, Atlanta
GA 30339-4024
Tel: (770) 433-8211
Web site: http://www.homedepot.com

DecoArt
P.O. Box 386, Stanford, KY 40484
Tel: (606) 365-3193
Web site: http://www.decoart.com

Stenciler's Emporium, Inc.
1325 Armstrong Road, Suite 170
Northfield, MN 55057
Tel: (800) 229-1760

Silver Brush Limited
92 Main Street, Bldg. 18C
Windsor, NJ 08561
Tel: (609) 443-4900
Fax: (609) 443-4888

Pearl Paint
308 Canal Street, New York, NY 10013
Tel: (212) 431-7931
Web site: http://www.pearlpaint.com

Hobby Lobby
7707 SW 44th Street, Oklahoma City
OK 73179
Tel: (405) 745-1100
Web site: http://www.hobbylobby.com

Michaels' Arts and Crafts
8000 Bent Branch Drive
Irving, TX 75063
Tel: (214) 409-1300
Web site: http://www. michaels.com

Unfinished furniture

Target Corporation
33S. Sixth Street, Minneapolis,
MN 55402
Tel: (800) 800-8800

Artcraft Wood Etc.
415E. Seventh Street, Joplin, MO
64801
Tel: (417) 782-7063
Fax: (417) 782-7064

Whittier Wood Products
P.O. Box 2827, Eugene, OR 97402
Tel: (541) 687-0213

Acknowledgements

Author's acknowledgements

Many, many thanks to Sue and Douglas Ronald for allowing us to photograph in their house. Special thanks to Liz Harris for her weekly enthusiastic, infectious and optimistic presence and to Lydia Banks for her very hardworking and timely work experience help.

Pamela Phillips-Minet commissioned me to paint two chairs and then was kind enough to lend them back to me for photography for which I am grateful. Thanks also to Mr and Mrs Hodson who kindly allowed us to photograph their kitchen and to Crick House Interiors (01869 343007) for the distressed and waxed cabinet on page 32 and the dresser on page 36. Thanks also to Julie Guicchiardi (0171 722 7414) for upholstering the chair on page 21.

Particular thanks go to the decorative painters who rallied to my help with furniture for this book:

Amy Dawson, Muralist and Specialist Painter
Tel: 0181 749 6636
pp. 18; 30; 33; 53 crackle varnish

Sally Grout-Smith, Paint Effects
Tel: 01798 344086
pp. 48 stripes, dragging; 46 freehand painting and crackle varnish

Hang-ups Accessories Ltd
Tel: 01285 831771
Showroom (viewing by appointment only)
Tel: 0171 371 2206
pp. 44–45 metallic wax, distressed gilding, gilding and freehand painting, dragging and metal leaf

François Lavenir
Tel: 0171 581 1083
p. 101 bottom right

Victoria Morland, contact Sue Beaumont
Tel: 01280 848097
pp. 42–43 painted tortoiseshell, coloured tortoiseshell, dragging and freehand lining, dragging and metallic paint and bird's-eye maple; 54–55 red tortoiseshell, marble effect and metallic effects

Valerie Traynor, Decorative Artist
Tel: 001 978 369 3440
pp. 21 right; 23 left; 27 right; 55 distressed gilding
I am indebted to Valerie Traynor for her advice on the sky painting technique.

Nicola Wingate-Saul of Nicola Wingate-Saul Print Rooms
Tel and fax: 01323 871195
pp. 28 right, 35, 112–113

Picture credits

The author and publishers would like to thank the following sources for their kind permission to reproduce the photographes listed:

Elizabeth Whiting Associates: p. 6 (Di Lewis/Mary Rose Young); p. 8 (Andrew Kolesnikow); p. 9T&B (Tom Leighton); p. 12R.

Abode: p. 10 (Trevor Richards); p. 11T (Trevor Richards); p. 11B (Ian Parry); p. 12L (Ian Parry); p. 13 (Ian Parry).